THE YOUNG HEGELIANS
AND KARL MARX

McLELLAN, David. The Young Hegelians and Karl Marx. Praeger, 1969. 170p bibl 76-90413. 8.50

CHOICE　　*APR.'70*

Philosophy

Although rather expensive for its size, McLellan's volume is a welcome addition to a very sparse field. The only full scale study in English devoted exclusively to the Young Hegelians, it takes its place beside Sidney Hook's *From Hegel to Marx* (1950) and Löwith's *From Hegel to Nietzsche* (CHOICE, Nov. 1964). The chapters devoted to Bauer, Feuerbach, Stirner, and Hess make this book an indispensable tool for American students of 19th-century German thought interested in the origins of Marx' philosophy. The relation of the Young Hegelians to Hegel and Marx' development during the *Deutsch-französische Jahrbücher* period are thoroughly and lucidly treated. However, the chapter on Stirner is too brief and superficial to be of important use. A fuller and more penetrating treatment of Stirner is found in Löwith's more philosophically sophisticated volume. McLellan, a product of Oxford and Frankfurt, is a lecturer in politics and government at the University of Kent at Canterbury. Recommended.

THE AUTHOR: David McLellan was educated at Merchant Taylors' School and St. John's College, Oxford. After studying in Paris and Frankfurt, he returned to Oxford to finish his doctorate, and he is now a lecturer in politics and government at the University of Kent at Canterbury.

THE
YOUNG HEGELIANS
AND KARL MARX

DAVID McLELLAN

FREDERICK A. PRAEGER, *Publishers*

New York · Washington

BOOKS THAT MATTER

Published in the United States of America in 1969
by Frederick A. Praeger, Inc., Publishers
111 Fourth Avenue, New York, N.Y. 10003
© 1969 in London, England, by David McLellan
Library of Congress Catalog Card Number: 76-90413

Printed in Great Britain

TO
SIMONE BRASSART

CONTENTS

INTRODUCTION

BRUNO BAUER

PREFACE

The following studies are intended to fill what is an increasingly evident gap in the history of ideas. The disciples of Hegel, even the radical ones, inevitably shared the eclipse of their Master, but the recent strong revival of interest in Hegel justifies a fresh look at his followers. The period has attracted attention lately owing to the publication of some of Marx's early writings and the ensuing discussions of them. In these discussions mention of the ideas of Marx's Young Hegelian contemporaries only occurs by the way. Here I have reversed the emphasis, believing both that the thought of the leading Young Hegelians is important in itself and also that the understanding of the genesis of Marx's ideas would be made easier by an extended study of the intellectual climate of his youth.

I would like to thank Sir Isaiah Berlin and Professor James Joll for much generous help; also Professors Theodor Adorno and Iring Fetscher of the University of Frankfurt. Needless to say, I alone am responsible for remaining deficiencies. Finally, I would like to thank St John's College, Oxford, for continued kind hospitality.

D. M.

Littlecroft,
Chilham,
Kent
January 1968

INTRODUCTION

1. The Beginnings of the Hegelian School

a. *The School after Hegel's Death*

In the years immediately following the death of Hegel in 1831, his disciples continued to present as united a front as they had during the lifetime of the Master.[1] Hegel's philosophy had become supreme in Germany during the 1820s, being strongly supported by the Minister of Culture, Altenstein, and found its focal point in the *Berliner-Kritische Association* which started in 1827 to produce the Hegelian periodical *Jahrbücher für wissenschaftliche Kritik*. Early in 1832 a union was formed of seven of Hegel's most intimate friends and pupils, most of them from Berlin, which continued to be the intellectual centre of the School, to propagate Hegel's teaching and to prepare a complete edition of his works, including all the lectures. The general view was that Hegel's philosophy was the ultimate one and that all that was left for his pupils to do was to work out its implications in the various fields as yet only touched upon by Hegel himself. One of the seven editors of Hegel's complete works, Gans, wrote in an obituary notice that 'philosophy has now come full circle; its progress is only to be considered as the thoughtful working over of its material in the manner which the lately departed has so clearly and precisely indicated'.[2] Another of the seven, Förster, likened the philosophical situation to the empire of Alexander: no successor could mount the throne, but various satraps would divide the provinces between themselves. As if to emphasise this, Hegel's chair was occupied by the colourless Gabler.

---

[1] L. Michelet, *Geschichte der letzten Systeme der Philosophie in Deutschland von Kant bis Hegel* (Berlin, 1837) ii, p. 636.

[2] E. Gans, *Vermischte Schriften* (Berlin, 1834) pp. 251f.

Inevitably, however, differences of opinion began to appear and arguments began to break out inside the School. People started to ask whether Hegel was not really a pantheist and the two questions most hotly debated were the immortality of the soul and the personality of God, questions that had already been raised before Hegel's death by Feuerbach in his anonymous book *Gedanken über Tod und Unsterblichkeit*. The scope for debate was all the larger since the verbal tradition of Hegel's teaching was extremely varied and even Hegel's written works on the subject were rather ambiguous.[1] Hegel time and time again referred to Christianity as the 'absolute' and 'perfect' religion. For him, philosophy and religion had the same content, the only difference was that philosophy made explicit what religion apprehended by means of imagination and pictures. The reality was the same: only the mode of perception differed. Hegel's intention was to show that philosophy and religion were reconcilable and thus to refute rationalist critics of the Kantian type while at the same time attacking the supernatural theologians who believed in a philosophically unprovable revelation and also the disciples of Schleiermacher who confounded intellectual distinctions 'by suppressing the discriminating concept and by establishing the "feeling" of the essence, promoting not so much insight as edification'.[2] On the other hand, Hegel did sometimes use forms of words that suggested he conceived of God's knowledge of himself simply as man's self-consciousness – a theme later taken up by the Young Hegelians. This ambiguity was not brought out into the open during the lifetime of Hegel who considered himself an orthodox Lutheran.[3]

The differences inside the Hegelian School were brought more into evidence in 1835 by D. F. Strauss with his book *Das Leben Jesu*. Strauss had been educated at Tübingen as a pupil of the radical Old Testament critic F. C. Baur and came to Berlin to attend Hegel's lectures just before his death. Unlike Hegel, who

[1] L. Michelet, op. cit. ii, p. 638.

[2] G. Hegel, *Werke* (Berlin, 1832ff.) ii, p. 8.

[3] The two books recently published in English on Hegel by Findlay and Kaufmann are extremely one-sided on this point, labelling Hegel as a – perhaps unconscious – atheist on the basis of one or two texts and ignoring others.

had treated the historicity of the Gospels as a comparatively unimportant question and concentrated on a speculative interpretation of their symbolic content, Strauss considered that the Gospel narratives were the essence of the Christian religion and treated them not as symbols but as myths translating the profound desires of the people.

The Gospels were for him imaginations of facts produced by the collective consciousness of a people who had arrived at a specific stage of development. This implied that the revelation and incarnation of the divine essence could not be limited to one individual and that its sole adequate field was the whole of humanity. The effect of Strauss's book was immediate and profound. Rudolf Haym, later one of the most prominent liberal philosophers of the mid-century, described its impact thus:

> It was Strauss's *Das Leben Jesu* that both filled me and a number of my companions with Hegelian attitudes and also made us more and more disillusioned with theology. The spell that this book exercised over one was indescribable; I never read any book with so much pleasure and thoroughness. . . . It was as though scales fell from my eyes and a great light was shed on my path.[1]

Strauss's book did not create the divisions among Hegel's disciples – for they had always been there – but it did accentuate them, for he came under attack not only from the orthodox Lutherans, led by Hengstenberg, professor of theology at Berlin, but also from the followers of Hegel who wished to defend the Master's reconciliation of philosophy and religion. It was Strauss himself who coined the expression that later became attached to the various parties, dividing them into left, right and centre, borrowing this from the current description of the French parliament. After emphasising the obscurity of Hegel's view of the matter, Strauss wrote.

> To the question whether and how far the Gospel history is contained as history in the idea of the unity of divine and human nature, there are three possible answers: namely that from this concept either the whole Gospel narrative or only a part of it

---

[1] R. Haym, *Aus meinem Leben* (Berlin, 1902) pp. 105f.

or finally that neither the whole of it nor a part of it can be deduced as history from the idea. If these three answers or directions were each represented by a branch of the Hegelian School, then one could, following the traditional simile, call the first direction the right, as the one standing nearest to the old system, the third left and the second the centre.[1]

It should be emphasised that the existence of a centre – represented according to Strauss by Rosenkranz – showed that there was no very clear division between the parties. Bruno Bauer, a young lecturer in theology at the University of Berlin, who had been chosen to write the official review of Strauss's book in the *Jahrbücher für wissenschaftliche Kritik*, was after a year or two found leading the attack from the left. Also the divisions of opinion on purely religious topics were by no means the same when, in following years, political questions came to the forefront: Eduard Gans was reckoned by Strauss as belonging to the right wing, but was nevertheless the chief propagandist of Saint-Simonian ideas in Germany, and Strauss himself proved a thorough-going conservative years later during the troubles of 1848. These arguments about religion are nevertheless important as the fore-runners of later political divisions some of which never quite escaped from the influence of their origins.

b. *Social and Economic Background*

Before going on to trace the development of the Hegelian School and the gradual emergence of a political opposition, it might be as well to say something about the intellectual and social background in the various provinces of Germany. Prussia, and particularly Berlin, was the home ground of Hegelianism. Bruno Bauer complained that the Berliners themselves were unpolitically minded – they were mostly court officials and small merchants – but the university had the best reputation in Germany. For Rosenkranz the atmosphere in Berlin was one where criticism flourished, full of intellectual curiosity and gossip, while Feuerbach wrote home to his father that 'in no other university does such general in-

[1] D. Strauss, *Streitschriften* (Tübingen, 1841) iii, p. 95.

dustry rule, such striving for knowledge, such peace and quiet as here'.[1]

The discussions in Berlin did not as yet have the political overtones that already existed in East Prussia, where the influence of Kant, centred on the University of Königsberg, where he had had his chair, was supreme. Kant's doctrine of the autonomy of the moral person led to a demand that all members of the state should participate in the government and to a constitutional movement that culminated in 1841 in the liberal pamphlet of Johann Jacoby *Vier Fragen beantwortet von einem Ostpreussen Preussen.* This opposition was led by the president von Schön and supported by the large land-owners who admired English methods of government and complained that nothing was done to help the critical state of agriculture.

If the liberalism of East Prussia looked to England for its model, that in South-West Germany was more inspired by French examples. The movement was led by two teachers of the University of Freiburg, Rotteck and Welcher, who, while not democrats, wished to see a separation of powers and the sovereignty of the law. Their most influential publication was the *Staatslexikon* and the political life was comparatively well developed there, as the states of the South-West had constitutions and provincial assemblies open to political debate.

The most advanced industrially of the German provinces at this time was undoubtedly the Rhineland. Nearly twenty years of French occupation had given its inhabitants a knowledge of Republican institutions that they did not forget and the anticatholic attitude of the Prussian government also tended to alienate the feelings of the population. Nevertheless in the late 1830s the growing benefits of the *Zollverein* persuaded the leading business men to favour collaboration with the Prussian authorities.[2]

[1] L. Feuerbach, *Briefwechsel* (Leipzig, 1963) p. 25.

[2] For more detail on the social background, see the excellent article by J. Droz and P. Ayçoberry, 'Structures sociales et courants idéologiques – Allemagne prérévolutionnaire', *Annali*, VI, pp. 164–236.

2. The Young Hegelians

a. General Characteristics

It was against this background that the Hegelian School developed. As has been indicated, the Old Hegelians tried to hold a middle course between the fundamentalism of Hengstenberg, professor of theology at Berlin and leader of the orthodox Lutherans, and the over-negative radicalism of Strauss and his followers. They wished to preserve Hegel's ideas of the reconciliation of philosophy and religion and confined themselves to an interpretation of what this involved. In philosophy, since they believed Hegel's system to be the final one, their work consisted mostly in writing the history of philosophy. In politics they held to the proposition that 'the real is the rational' and remained aloof, in the belief, according to Rosenkranz, that 'they should quietly take over Hegel's doctrines, avoid all extremes and, in the knowledge that their philosophy was world-historical, final and reconciling all contradictions, not get involved in the struggles of the moment: a position of positive quietism'.[1]

As for the Young Hegelians, it is impossible to speak of a 'movement' before about 1840, when the more and more radical position of the *Hallische Jahrbücher für deutsche Wissenschaft und Kunst*, their principal organ, provided a rallying-point. They were at the beginning exclusively preoccupied with religious questions and, as Ruge later remarked, the extent to which the origins of the Hegelian School were theological can be measured by the fact that it was the purely theological book of Strauss that had the most influence on its development. Apart from art and literature, religion was the only field where different alignments and relatively free debate were possible. Because of the censorship almost all newspapers were merely pale reflections of the government's views. Genuinely political arguments among the Young Hegelians did not appear before about 1840 when the accession of Frederick-William IV and the attendant relaxation of press censorship opened the newspapers for a short time to their propaganda.

The focal point of the Young Hegelians was the University of Berlin. Almost all of them – Bruno and Edgar Bauer, Cieszkowski,

[1] K. Rosenkranz, *Aus einem Tagebuch* (Leipzig, 1851) p. 47.

Feuerbach, Stirner, Marx and Engels – had studied philosophy in Berlin. Hess and Ruge were the only important exceptions. Several of them – Bruno and Edgar Bauer, Feuerbach, Ruge – had followed the example of Hegel in beginning their studies with theology, only later switching to philosophy. All came from well-to-do, middle-class families, such as could afford to send their sons to a university, for the Young Hegelians were an extremely intellectual group for which a university education was essential, Hess being the only self-educated member. Ruge's parents were landowners, the fathers of Feuerbach and Marx were both prosperous lawyers, those of Hess and Engels owned factories and even the flute-making and porcelain painting of the fathers of Stirner and the Bauer brothers made enough money to keep the family in easy circumstances. Apart from Hess and Engels, both to some extent autodidacts in philosophy since their fathers wished them to go into the family business, all the Young Hegelians wished to go in for teaching in some form or another, most of them in universities, though Köppen and Stirner taught in high schools. Their misfortune was that, owing to their unorthodox ideas, the universities were gradually closed to them and they found themselves without a job and cut off from society. Feuerbach early gave up hope of a university career. His father had warned him that his first book, *Gedanken* published in 1832, would cost him the prospect of a chair. Ruge was given to understand in 1837 that he could not expect a professorship and their last hopes were destroyed when, in 1842, Bruno Bauer, through whom Marx had hoped to obtain a philosophical post at the University of Bonn, was even deprived of his *licentia docendi*.

With this background it is not surprising that the Young Hegelians should put such emphasis on the role of ideas and theory. They were in origin a philosophical School and their approach to religion and politics was always intellectual. Their philosophy is best called a speculative rationalism; for to their romantic and idealist elements they added the sharp critical tendencies of the *Aufklärung* and an admiration for the principles of the French Revolution. The second half of Feuerbach's *Das Wesen des Christentums* was full of the old *Aufklärung* arguments against religion, Bruno and Edgar Bauer made long historical studies of the French Revolution, as did Marx also, and the

Young Hegelians in general were very fond of comparing themselves either to the 'mountain' or to individual revolutionaries of
that time. They believed in reason as a continually unfolding
process and conceived it their task to be its heralds. They
radicalised still further Hegel's conception of religion as a prelude
to philosophy by denying the possibility of any supernatural
revelation.

Like Hegel, they believed that the process would achieve an
ultimate unity but they tended – especially Bruno Bauer – to
believe that it would be immediately preceded by an ultimate
division. This meant that some of their writings had a very
apocalyptic ring, for they thought it their duty by their criticism
to force divisions to a final rupture and thus to their complete
resolution.

The sometimes fantastic views of the Young Hegelians, views
that Marx was later led to call mockingly 'pregnant with world
revolution',[1] were helped firstly by their impression that they
lived in an age of transition and at the dawn of a completely new
era. Metternich in his old age described in a striking fashion in
his diary the age of which he refused to approve: 'Profound
reflection leads me to think that the old Europe is at the beginning of its end . . . on the other hand, the new Europe is still in
gestation; between the beginning and the end there will be a
chaos'.[2] Hegel, too, in the preface to his *Phänomenologie des
Geistes* said that the age in which he wrote was a time of transition
and birth of a new period; spirit was at work giving itself a new
form.[3] Their apocalyptic tendencies were increased by their
position as jobless intellectuals on the marge of society. Having
no roots in the society that they were criticising, they could allow
their ideas to range at will. Secondly, the Young Hegelians
placed great faith in the power of ideas: here again Bauer was the
most outstanding example. Heine had already said that thought
preceded action as lightning did thunder, and this was taken up
most forcibly by Ludwig Buhl, editor of one of the Young
Hegelians' very short-lived periodicals in Berlin: 'Have you

---

[1] K. Marx and F. Engels, *Gesamtausgabe* (Berlin, 1927 ff.) I, i. 2,
p. 285. (Hereafter referred to as *MEGA*.)

[2] Metternich, *Nachgelassene Papiere* (Berlin 1880–4), III, p. 348.

[3] G. Hegel, *Werke* (Berlin, 1832 ff.) II, p. 10.

learnt', he wrote, 'so little from history that you do not realise that theory always precedes new action as John the Baptist did Christ? Theory blazes the trail and prepares the arrival of the new Messiah. Christianity was a theory, the Reformation was a theory, the Revolution a theory: they have become actions.'[1] It was precisely on this 'trail-blazing' that the Young Hegelians were engaged. Marx echoed this thought in his first piece of serious writing, the doctoral dissertation of 1841, when he wrote, following Bruno Bauer, that even the practice of philosophy was itself theoretical.[2] Even when some of the Young Hegelians began to express their ideas in purely political terms, this idea of the independence and primacy of theory still held sway. As late as 1843, Marx could still write that 'theory is capable of becoming a practical force when it seizes the masses',[3] a view shared by Ruge's comment that praxis was 'the movement of the masses in the direction of theory'.[4]

b. *Transition from Thought to Action – August von Cieszkowski*

Despite, however, their faith in the power of ideas, there increased during the late 1830s the vague feeling that this was no longer enough. The first writer to give this feeling a precise formulation was August von Cieszkowski. Cieszkowski was born in 1814, the son of a Polish count, and after studying philosophy in Warsaw had gone to Berlin in 1832, where he stayed for three years, becoming a pupil and lifelong friend of the orthodox Hegelian Michelet. In 1838, after a period of travelling, he published in German a small book entitled *Prolegomena zur Historiosophie*. Cieszkowski's main object in writing the book was to replace speculative philosophy by a philosophy that brought practical action within its reach. It was not enough, according to him, to discover the laws of past history, men must use this knowledge to change the world in the future. Hegel had divided world history into three periods, the oriental, the Graeco-Roman and the Germano-Christian: for Cieszkowski, antiquity was the first

---

[1] L. Buhl, *Der Beruf der preussischen Presse* (Berlin, 1842) p. 4.
[2] K. Marx, *Frühe Schriften*, I, p. 71.   [3] Ibid. p. 497.
[4] A. Ruge, *Zwei Jahre in Paris*, II, p. 134.

period, the second stretched from Christ to Hegel and the third was yet to come. With Hegel philosophy had reached its culmination, his absolute idealism had achieved everything that philosophy was capable of and was 'the long awaited discovery of the alchemist's stone'.[1] But this was not enough: Hegel's deficiencies were the deficiencies of philosophy itself. For his philosophy could only explain history *post factum*, could only contemplate what had happened or was happening and was in no position to extend itself to a conscious shaping of the future. Parallel with his three periods Cieszkowski considered that there were three successive ways of determining the future: the first by feeling, appropriate to the seer, the second by knowledge, appropriate to the philosopher, the third was 'truly practical, applied, complete, spontaneous, willed and free, thus embracing the whole sphere of action'.[2] Cieszkowski's aim was to 'vindicate for speculation knowledge of the essence of the future'.[3] Cuvier had been able to reconstruct the whole anatomy of a beast from a single tooth: it was the philosopher's job to construct out of past epochs of history its ideal totality and particularly the future, though Cieszkowski only claimed by his science to be able to deduce the essence of the future, not its particulars – it was *praesagium*, not *praescientia*. He followed his Master in thinking that his age was the age of crisis and transition *par excellence*. However, the deep divisions and contradictions in man's consciousness would ultimately be resolved into a final unity and the method Cieszkowski proposed for this resolution was 'historiosophy'. The main agent in this transformation was not to be thought, as in Hegel's philosophy, but will, which was the motive force for that synthesis of thought and action for which Cieszkowski coined the term, so influential later, of 'praxis'. The future role of philosophy was 'to become a practical philosophy or rather a philosophy of practical activity, of "praxis", exercising a direct influence on social life and developing the future in the realm of concrete activity'.[4] This would mean, Cieszkowski claimed, that future history would be one of acts and not of facts. Here Cieszkowski, like the Young Hegelians after him, is nearer to Fichte than to Hegel. Fichte constantly opposed thought, con-

[1] A. v. Cieszkowski, *Prolegomena* (Berlin, 1838) pp. 130f.
[2] Ibid. p. 16.   [3] Ibid. p. 8.   [4] Ibid. p. 129.

ceived by him as will in action, to present reality and considered its main task was to determine the future.

Cieszkowzski had stayed in Paris for the two years immediately before he wrote his book and the activist political tradition there had certainly influenced him a lot. Socialist ideas in particular had left a great impression on him. He singled out Fourier for special attention and recommended a study of his works to his fellow Hegelians. Fourier's system was 'a considerable step forward on the path to the concrete realisation of organic truth' and 'one important stage in the formation of true reality'.[1] He was, however, in the eyes of Cieszkowski, too utopian, contrasting the present situation with a future thought out *a priori* and not establishing the essential bridge between the two. Saint Simon also seems materially to have influenced Cieszkowski's books: Cieszkowski puts considerable emphasis on the importance of the relations of production in all future development, as did Saint Simon who was also convinced of the possibility of predicting the future course of events. Cieszkowski also talks of the atomisation of society, of selfishness and the aristocracy of wealth in the same terms that Hess uses a little later.

Though there is no evidence that Cieszkowski's book was very widely read, yet it certainly came to the notice of Herzen, who was overjoyed on reading it to find himself in agreement with Cieszkowski on all essential points.[2] Hess refers to the *Prolegomena* often and borrows considerably from it, and its emphasis on a philosophy of action was as prophetic for the Young Hegelians in politics as Strauss's book had been in religion. Thus it was Cieszkowski who gave the first impetus to the process of swift secularisation that set in among the Young Hegelians in the next few years.

c. *Foundation of the 'Hallische Jahrbücher' and the Beginnings of the Young Hegelian Movement*

Cieszkowski's book also received an enthusiastic notice in the

---

[1] Ibid. pp. 146, 148.
[2] Cf. A. Koyré, *Études sur l'histoire de la pensée philosophique en Russie* (Paris, 1950) pp. 188 ff.

Hallische Jahrbücher and it was around this review and its successor, the *Deutsche Jahrbücher*, that the Young Hegelian movement centred. Its editors were two teachers at the University of Halle, Theodor Echtermeyer and Arnold Ruge. The first idea for the review came from the former, but the drive and enthusiasm from the latter. Ruge was born in 1802 on the north coast of Prussia. He had thought of doing theology, but eventually turned to philosophy which he studied at Halle. The earnestness and semi-puritanism that stayed with him all his life compelled him to join in an obscure conspiracy of the *Burschenschaften* whose discovery caused him to be sent to prison for six years. On his liberation in 1830 he started lecturing on Plato at the University of Halle, then read Hegel and became a disciple. His wife was rich and so, when the government refused to give him a chair, he ceased teaching and threw himself into editing the *Hallische Jahrbücher* with all his energy. For this he was admirably suited: he wrote quickly, had a large stock of suitable expressions and could turn them out elegantly. He described himself as a 'wholesale merchant in the realm of ideas' and, though no very original mind himself, stood at the centre of the Young Hegelian movement.

In its inception, the aims of the *Hallische Jahrbücher* were very broad. In a letter of August 1837 Ruge summed up their intentions as 'independent, genuine criticism from a scientific point of view together with an accurate account of the problems engaging contemporary minds'.[1] A few days later in a letter to Rosenkranz he described the future journal as 'a sort of contemporary hand on the clock of German literary and artistic life, characterising important personalities, reviewing different directions and fields in artistic matters and corresponding with other universities'.[2] It was intended for a wider public than the specialist journals, being readily comprehensible to any educated person and, appearing daily, fulfilled the need later answered by the literary supplements in newspapers.

At the end of 1837 Ruge made a long journey visiting universities far and wide from Göttingen to Tübingen and obtained as many as 159 contributors for the *Jahrbücher*. The original breadth of opinion among the contributors is shown by the fact

[1] A. Ruge, *Briefwechsel*, I, p. 66.   [2] Ibid. p. 67.

that even the arch-pietist Leo was represented by one essay.
During the first few months the journal was almost exclusively
devoted to literary subjects. However, the principles of the
journal, described by Ruge in an editorial at the beginning of its
second year as 'protestantism and academic freedom as realised in
a protestant and modern state',[1] soon brought a good deal of
criticism, for the review defended Strauss and in its support of free
criticism was noticeably anti-clerical. The episode that really
gave the review a political turn and drew upon it the criticism
that forced it into opposition was the quarrel which opposed the
Archbishop of Cologne to the Prussian government on the question of mixed marriages. The previous archbishop had dispensed
non-Catholic partners in mixed marriages from the promises in
theory demanded of them by Rome. His successor decided to
apply the papal instruction strictly, was arrested in November
1837 and only released after the death of Frederick-William III in
1840. The smouldering discontent caused by the government's
action was fanned into a blaze by a brilliant tract of political
propaganda written by Görres, a professor at Munich University,
defending the ultramontane position. The argument was so
intense that more than 300 pamphlets were produced for or
against Görres. The most prominent among the pamphleteers
was Heinrich Leo, too good a protestant and too fond of controversy not to take up the gauntlet that Görres had cast down. But
his conservatism made him sympathetic to Görres's position on
many points and this showed in his reply. Ruge reviewed Leo's
brochure in the *Jahrbücher* and the review was, in his own words,
'angry and thundering',[2] specifically appealing to the principles
of the Reformation and the *Aufklärung*. Leo's reply was no less
violent, resuming in the following four points the charges he
brought against the Young Hegelians:

1. This party denies any sort of a personal God ... this party
   openly teaches atheism.
2. This party openly teaches that the Gospel is mythology.
3. This party openly teaches a purely terrestrial religion.
4. Moreover, this party by covering its impious and sacrilegious

[1] A. Ruge, *Sämtliche Werke*, I, p. 7.
[2] A. Ruge, *Briefwechsel*, I, p. 131.

doctrines with a repugnant and abstruse phraseology does not hesitate to give itself the appearance of a Christian party.[1]

This argument cost the *Jahrbücher* some of its contributors and a consequent narrowing of its point of view. In September 1838 Witte withdrew owing to attacks on Leo and Erdmann, and in November, Raumer also withdrew giving as a reason that the *Jahrbücher* had attacked Christianity.[2]

The early essays in the *Jahrbücher*, especially Ruge's, were all favourable to the Prussian state and in his contribution to the Görres–Leo controversy he went out of his way to glorify it. In this field the disciples remained faithful to the Master and were only forced to alter their views by the authorities' attitude to their teaching on different subjects, particularly religious. As late as November 1839, in an article in the *Jahrbücher* entitled 'Protestantismus und Romantik', while deploring the Romanticism that was responsible for certain reactionary trends in Prussia, Ruge was yet able to put the accent on an appeal from Prussia drunk with Romanticism, to Prussia sober and imbued with the principles of liberalism. However, by the end of 1839 the *Jahrbücher* had begun to go in for essays of a directly political character, a course that was implicit in the logic of the situation, for an attack on orthodox religion was, at least in the eyes of the Prussian government, an attack upon the 'Christian state'. In his first essay of directly political criticism Ruge wrote that Prussia 'is at the present moment in her profound tendencies and constitution essentially Catholic'.

It was at this time that Ruge and the *Jahrbücher* began to be stimulated in their political criticism by the Berlin Young Hegelians, the centre of whom was a group known as the *Doktorklub*. The club was formed as a discussion group for radical Hegelians and was in existence by 1837, for it was largely through discussions with its members that Marx was converted to Hegelianism.[3] He wrote in a letter home to his father:

[1] H. Leo, *Die Hegelingen* (Halle, 1838) pp. 2f.

[2] A. Ruge, *Briefwechsel*, I, pp. 144, 152.

[3] There is no evidence whatever that Marx was 'the central figure' in the club, as Rubel alleges (*Karl Marx*, Paris, 1957, p. 28).

Through several meetings with friends in Stralow I gained access to a Post-Doctoral Club whose members included several lecturers and my most intimate Berlin friend Dr. Rutenberg. In the discussion here many contradictory views came to light and I attached myself even closer to the modern view of the world.[1]

The members were university lecturers and school teachers who did a bit of journalism in their spare time and also a few students like Marx. Rutenberg, whom Marx mentions in his letter, taught in a Berlin secondary school and wrote regularly in the liberal Hamburg newspaper *Der Telegraph*. Karl Köppen, another close friend of Marx at this time, also taught in a grammar school and had produced a book on the origins of Buddhism. Eduard Meyen and Ludwig Buhl had just completed their doctorates and earned their living by journalism. Since the club had no regular meetings or membership it is impossible to form any clear impression of it. No doubt, as Marx's descriptions seem to indicate, there were many differences of opinion, and Bruno Bauer, who was later to be its central figure, held to an orthodox Hegelian position throughout most of 1839. It seems to have ceased its activities when Bauer went to Bonn in 1841 and to have been restarted under the name of the *Freien* when Bauer returned to Berlin after his dismissal.

Up to the end of the 1830s the political attitude of the Young Hegelians was one of loyal opposition: they believed that their ideals could be realised within the framework of the Prussian state. But in the spring of 1840 both Frederick-William III and his Minister Altenstein, who had been favourable to the Hegelians, died. The new king's character was very different from that of his father. Affable and unreliable, he was imbued with a Christian Romanticism that idealised the past and particularly the Restoration governments. He hated the ideas of the French Revolution and of the *Aufklärung*. A slow development of old traditions was his ideal, a government based on provincial estates in the traditional German patriarchal spirit. He was, moreover, a convinced pietist and opposed to liberalism. He believed that as a king he was enlightened in a special way by God and con-

[1] K. Marx, *Frühe Schriften*, I, p. 15.

ceived it to be his mission to instil into his people an attitude that
more closely resembled his own type of Christianity.
Nevertheless at the time of his accession the Young Hegelians
were hopeful. Bruno Bauer, in a history of this time written a
few years later, said: 'A dawn of hope is reflected on everyone's
face and brightens their looks and from all hearts a great joy
seems continually to spring'.[1] Typical of this enthusiasm was the
brochure by Karl Köppen entitled *Friedrich der Grosse und seine
Widersacher*, which he dedicated to Karl Marx. Köppen gave a
very idealised portrait of Frederick II as the philosopher king who
had nurtured the principles of the *Aufklärung* in Prussia. The
burden of the book was that the future of Prussia depended on a
continuing fidelity to these principles: 'heaven rests no more
surely upon the shoulders of Atlas than does Prussia on the
development, adapted to the needs of our age, of the principles of
Frederick the Great'.[2]

d. The 'Rheinische Zeitung'

The first measures of the new King seemed to justify these hopes.
There was an amnesty for political prisoners, the publication of
the proceedings of provincial diets was permitted and a commis-
sion uniting all the provincial diets was to meet every two years
in Berlin. Most important of all, there was to be a relaxation in
the press censorship. The instruction of 1819 that 'no earnest
and circumspect search after truth is to be hindered' had not
been respected by the censors and the new edict corrected this.
The edict was promulgated in December 1841 and had as an
immediate effect the founding of the *Rheinische Zeitung*, a newspaper that soon became notorious as a more popular counterpart
of the *Hallische Jahrbücher*. Originally the foundation of the
Rheinische Zeitung was favoured by the government as providing
an opposition to the *Kölnische Zeitung*, a paper noted for its

[1] B. Bauer, *Vollständige Geschichte der Parteikämpfe in Deutschland*
(Charlottenburg, 1847) I, p. 5.
[2] K. Köppen, *Friedrich der Grosse* (Leipzig, 1840) p. 171. For a vivid
portrait of Frederick-William IV see Marx's letter to Ruge in *Frühe
Schriften*, pp. 436ff.

ultramontanism which at that time had a monopoly of the Catholic Rhineland. The new paper was also supported by many of the liberal-minded business men who wanted an organ to press for a customs union with Prussia. From the beginning, however, a more radical element had been present. The two directors of the paper, Oppenheim and Jung, were radical followers of Hegel and friends of Moses Hess, who, having just finished the first book to gain him public recognition, *Die Europäische Triarchie*, was the man chiefly responsible for organising support for the paper. He had hoped to be made editor, but his views were considered too extreme and he had to accept a position subordinate to Höffken, a disciple of the liberal economist List. Within a month Höffken resigned in protest at the directors' interfering with the running of the newspaper and declaring himself 'no disciple of Young Hegelianism'.[1] However, he was replaced by Rutenberg, one of the Berlin Young Hegelians recently dismissed from his teaching post for the propagation of subversive opinions. He opened his columns to the Young Hegelians who, helped by an exceptionally lax censorship, became the chief contributors to the paper. According to one of the later censors 'the editors, entering into relations with the *Freien* in Berlin defended ... with growing audacity the ideas of the Hegelian left, openly proclaiming as a political dogma the necessity of destroying the Church and establishing a constitution and absolute liberty of the press'.[2]

The period from the accession of Frederick-William IV until the end of 1842 and the suppression of the radical press was the time when the Young Hegelian movement was at its greatest strength. Still fully confident in the truth of their doctrines and anticipating their increasing effectiveness, they had no idea how rapidly their movement would dissolve when it came upon practical opposition. The next few sections are devoted to examining certain aspects of the Young Hegelians' thought during these years.

[1] J. Hansen, *Rheinische Briefe und Akten zur Geschichte der politischen Bewegung*, I, p. 316.
[2] Ibid. p. 467.

e. *The Young Hegelians and Hegel's Dialectic*

The disciples' attitude to their Master was always ambivalent.
Everyone agreed that Hegel's system was the last possible one.
He had, according to Ruge, systematised all previous philosophical thinking and his system was the culmination of Protestantism, as Protestantism was the culmination of Christianity:
his philosophy was 'the theory of all previous history and thus at
the same time its critique'.[1] All the other Young Hegelians,
including Feuerbach and Marx, said the same thing in their own
ways. Their energies were devoted to realising their inheritance,
making it effective and relevant to their own situation. According to Engels, they left Hegel's system on one side and concentrated on employing his dialectic, first on religious and then
on political problems; and Ruge said some years later that the
critique, or dialectical method, of the Young Hegelians was
always a 'Hegelian' critique.[2] This is, however, inaccurate: in
reality the Young Hegelians gradually turned Hegel's dialectic,
to which the concept of mediation was essential, into one which
held all mediation to be anathema. In his argument with Leo,
Ruge already spoke of an 'absolute negation', an expression that
Hegel would never have used in this context. At first this utter
negation was limited to extreme attitudes (Catholic reaction,
Romanticism) and a truly dialectical evolution was thought to be
possible elsewhere. But the worsening political situation soon
altered this and the Hegelian notion of a compromise mediated
between two opposing poles gave place to the idea of two contradictory parties, one of which must triumph utterly. This idea
was particularly developed by Edgar Bauer in his polemics
against those who favoured the liberal policies of a *juste milieu*,
and reached its complete expression in an article written by
Bakunin for the *Deutsche Jahrbücher* in 1842. Bakunin had been
in Germany since 1840 and wrote his article while at Dresden
where he had got to know Ruge. Negation was for Bakunin
creative: 'the positive is opposed by the negative and the
negative by the positive . . . the negative is only justified in its
absolute form'. He went on to attack the party of mediators as

[1] A. Ruge, *Zwei Jahre in Paris*, ii, p. 27.
[2] Ibid. p. 151.

being irreconcilable with the dialectical movement of history. The revolutionary spirit had already broken out once in France and it was about to do so again. Bakunin finished his article with the words: 'the joy of destruction is also a creative joy'.[1]

This was the final break with Hegel. But however far the disciples had moved from the spirit of Hegel's philosophy, they still considered themselves within his tradition and preferred to accuse the Master of compromise or even of concealing his principles in accordance with the political situation. Marx, in his dissertation, defended Hegel on this point, saying that 'if a philosopher has in fact yielded to expediency, his disciples ought to explain by means of his most profound ideas what took for him the form of exoteric thought'.[2] This difference between an 'esoteric' and an 'exoteric' Hegel was the most common formula under which the Young Hegelians dealt with the ideas of the Master. Hegel, either intentionally or not, had concealed the true meaning of his philosophy during his lifetime. The revolutionary tendencies of Hegel's thought were hidden and it was his disciples' task to bring them out into the open. The *locus classicus* for this idea is *Die Posaune des Jüngsten Gerichts über Hegel den Atheisten und Antichristen*, written by Bruno Bauer in 1841 pretending to be a devout pietist unmasking an 'atheistic' Hegel. The most consistent critic of Hegel was Ruge: from 1840 onwards one of the major themes of the *Hallische Jahrbücher* was a criticism of the 'self-sufficient thought of Hegel-brahmins'. In the preface to the first number of the *Deutsche Jahrbücher* Ruge, thinking no doubt of Hegel's preface to his *Rechtsphilosophie*, said that 'for Hegel philosophy was an ending with no room left for an "ought", it was simply the termination of a period'. The *Jahrbücher* waged a long campaign against Romanticism which was equated with reaction and, according to Ruge, Hegel 'unites in himself both romantic and free elements. Progress therefore consists in the cleansing of the Hegelian philosophy as achieved in the modern critical movement.'[3] Indeed, after the failure of the *Jahrbücher*, Ruge came to the position where he declared that 'in its true content the Hegelian philosophy of spirit is humanism.

[1] M. Bakunin, *Deutsche Jahrbücher* (1842) p. 1002.
[2] K. Marx, *Frühe Schriften*, pp. 70f.
[3] A. Ruge, *Sämtliche Werke*, I, p. 454.

c

In its true method it is criticism, the dissolution of all contradictions and fixed ideas.'[1] Hegel's close attention to empirical reality, his distaste for prediction, his dislike of ideas that were too dogmatic, the moderation and precision that the concept of mediation gave to the whole of his philosophy – all this was lacking in the Young Hegelians. Yet in their own minds and in their terminology, if not in their results, they considered themselves faithful disciples of Hegel to such an extent that Feuerbach, considered the most radical of his critics, was still able to write even in 1842 that 'everything is contained within Hegel's philosophy'.[2]

f. The Young Hegelians and Religion

The views of the Young Hegelians on religion underwent a considerable but consequent development during a very few years. Almost all their writings on religion are coloured by the political situation: they found it impossible to treat of religion separately from politics. To begin with, following Hegel, they tried to integrate religion into their view of the world, and gave their enthusiastic support to a certain form of Protestantism. In his above-mentioned manifesto in the *Jahrbücher* of 1839, entitled 'Protestantismus und Romantik', Ruge opposed a reactionary Romanticism to a liberal, Protestant view of Prussia. Two years later, taking a less optimistic view of the political situation, he opposed the Protestantism of Frederick the Great to the 'Catholic' policies of contemporary Prussia. This Protestantism, however, was never anything precise. Writing to Rosenkranz in 1840 Ruge said that for him 'Religion is merely incarnation . . . the pathos of the idea and devotion to it. And everyone is divine who achieves union with the idea'.[3] Strauss, according to him, was 'not liberal, not democratic enough'.[4] But by 1842 both Catholicism and Protestantism were condemned by Ruge as being incompatible with a liberal state.

[1] A. Ruge, *Zwei Jahre in Paris*, ii, pp. 122f.
[2] L. Feuerbach, *Sämtliche Werke*, ii, p. 227.
[3] A. Ruge, *Briefwechsel*, i, p. 203.
[4] Ibid.

It is important to realise what form of Christianity the Young Hegelians were attacking. The orthodox Lutherans tended to equate Christianity with a sort of biblical fundamentalism and also to have a typically pietist distrust of philosophy. When they talked about Christianity, all the Young Hegelians meant this form of pietism some of whose utterances completely justified their opponents' accusation of being anti-world and anti-nature. In addition some of the pietist groups were closely connected with the ultra-conservative Prussian nobility whose theoreticians were Ludwig von Gerlach and Stahl and who automatically distrusted any doctrine which, as did that of the Hegelians, subordinated the Church to the state.

Certain of the Berlin Young Hegelians – Stirner and Buhl, for example, – continued to proclaim a religion of humanity, but by the spring of 1842 they all followed the atheism proclaimed by Bruno Bauer in his *Die gute Sache der Freiheit*, published immediately after his dismissal from Bonn. And thereafter they constantly connected philosophy and atheism. Stirner wrote in the *Rheinische Zeitung*: 'To the philosopher, God is as indifferent as a stone: he is the complete atheist'.[1] Ruge's development was somewhat different: in 1842 he and his friend, the poet Georg Herwegh, heralded a 'new religion of humanity' and his position was much more ambiguous than that of the *Freien*. Rosenkranz says that the *Deutsche Jahrbücher* were suppressed *inter alia* for their denial of a supreme being, and in one of the final articles of the journal, 'Selbstkritik des Liberalismus', 1843, Ruge emphasised the necessity of secularising religion and the first point in his projected programme was 'to turn the churches into schools and organise therefrom a genuinely popular education system embracing all the masses'.[2] Yet in the same article he says that his programme would not involve the suppression of religion but its rebirth. He advocated a 'new idealism' that would turn counterfeit religion into genuine religion. For religion was in his view essential and without it no stone could be placed on another. Religion was the equivalent of freedom and Ruge remarked that in this respect they had progressed a long way since 1837 when so much attention had to be paid to the different views of the various

---

[1] M. Stirner, *Kleinere Schriften*, p. 45.
[2] A. Ruge, *Selbstkritik des Liberalismus*, *Sämtliche Werke*, iv, p. 114.

religious parties. In reality these differences did not represent
true religion: they were unpractical and incapable of setting the
masses in motion. Ruge's concepts at this time seem to have
been extremely confused. He began an account of these years by
remarking: 'I am not one of those who see liberation in a proclamation of atheism: atheism is as religious as Jacob struggling
with God'.[1] This ambiguity stems, of course, originally from
Hegel and was due particularly to Feuerbach who, in spite of his
apparent materialism, even claimed that his philosophy was
religion itself.

g. *The Young Hegelians and Politics*

Since in Germany at that time religion was so closely interwoven
with politics, it is not surprising that the Young Hegelians' views
on the state should parallel their views on religion and that both
should progressively incline towards what Hess called 'anarchism
in religion and politics'. Like their Master, the Young Hegelians
held an ideal view of the state, and particularly the Prussian state,
as the incarnation of objective morality. However, they considered that this ideal was not yet in being, but that in order to
realise it Prussia had only to continue the development begun
with the Reformation and the *Aufklärung*. It was inevitable that
in time the Young Hegelians should come to believe that Prussia
was incapable of fulfilling the role that they had assigned to her,
but since they employed their critical powers first of all on religious
questions, their political views were at first very moderate and up
until 1842 or 1843 their typical approach to political questions
was to oppose an (ideal) state to the Church and to blame the
latter for their troubles.

At the time of the controversy with Leo, Ruge had seen
Prussia as the realisation of Hegel's views, a Protestant state
capable of rebutting the Catholic tendencies of his opponents.
In the late 1830s the Young Hegelians were definitely opposed to
revolution: they advocated reform in order to avoid it. Ruge
wrote in 1838 that 'if the state contains within itself, as does
Prussia, a reforming principle, then there is neither the necessity

[1] A. Ruge, *Zwei Jahre in Paris*, i, p. 8.

nor the possibility of a revolution'.[1] And according to Buhl a revolution was only to be feared when political parties were suppressed: their existence favoured more peaceable solutions.[2] Before the accession of Frederick-William IV the *Jahrbücher* had defended the Prussian monarchy as the most advanced form of government and one capable, if appropriate steps were taken, of avoiding the excesses of 1789. Bruno Bauer, in his first piece of political writing, held roughly the same view. Leo accused him of holding 'a modern form of republicanism and even democracy'[3] but Bauer was all in favour of the state, merely saying that it had been corrupted by the Church and that it was the task of philo-sophy to liberate it. Reason was too much of the essence of the state for it to be long in error. Everyone looked to the throne to show the way. Hess went even further than the other Young Hegelians: for him the state was the organ of the total emancipa-tion of man, and the Prussian state in particular was 'the founder and promoter of German freedom of spirit'.[4] Even in a long article written in 1841 'Der christliche Staat' Bruno Bauer held much the same position: the general will was concentrated in the prince and, the state being objective morality, the Church could not presume to control it, and moreover there was always room for a dialectical opposition inside it. But immediately after the relaxation of the press censorship their ideas changed very quickly. In Berlin among the *Freien*, Köppen and Buhl were the most prolific writers. Together with Ruge they began to advocate a constitutional democracy, though Köppen at least thought this compatible with monarchy. Marx's articles in the *Rheinische Zeitung* are in the same style. It is quite inaccurate to say that Marx here is 'almost entirely free of Hegelianism'.[5] In line with the rest of the Young Hegelians Marx defended the rational state against its falsifications and called it 'the great organism in which legal, moral and political freedom is to find its realisation'.[6] The state's task was to bring into order the opposing forces of

---

[1] A. Ruge, *Hallische Jahrbücher*, 27–28 July 1838.

[2] L. Buhl, *Der Beruf der preussischen Presse* (Berlin, 1842), *passim*.

[3] H. Leo, *Evangelische Kirchenzeitung* (1841) vol. 28, col. 272.

[4] M. Hess, *Aufsätze*, p. 138.

[5] M. Rubel, *Karl Marx*, pp. 42f.

[6] K. Marx, *Frühe Schriften*, I, p. 185.

what Hegel had called 'civil society'. The laws for Marx were 'positive illuminations, general norms in which freedom has won an impersonal, theoretical existence, independent of the arbitrariness of the individual'.[1] At the same time Marx combined with this a Jacobin view of the state – to realise the desires of an exploited people deprived of their rights.

Up until 1841 the Young Hegelians had abstained from criticising the Master's political, as distinct from his religious, views. As late as September 1841 Bruno Bauer, at a banquet in honour of Welcker, the liberal political theorist from Baden, had praised Hegel's political philosophy in a toast as surpassing in liberalism and audacity the views prevalent in Southern Germany.[2] However, the change was not long in coming: in 1842 Ruge published the first direct criticism of Hegel in this field, attacking his *Rechtsphilosophie* for confounding logical and historical categories, thus anticipating many of Marx's criticisms in the following year.

In all their thinking, and particularly in politics, the Young Hegelians were influenced by the French Revolution. Here they followed in the wake of the Young Germany movement and especially of Heine and Börne, frequently comparing themselves with the Encyclopaedists. As early as 1838 Leo had referred to the Young Hegelians as 'a new edition of the Encyclopaedists and the heroes of the French Revolution'. Progress, they thought, would only be achieved under the intellectual hegemony of France. The waves of anti-French feeling that followed claims for the left bank of the Rhine found little echo among the Young Hegelians. For Hess, France was the land of revolution and movement, the land of will. Of course later, Paris being the centre of socialist ideas, the influence of French thought became even greater when socialism began to spread in Germany.

The political philosophy of the Young Hegelians can be well described as 'philosophical radicalism'. As such they were distinct from the much more widespread liberal movement. Liberalism, being a movement with a large amount of at least tacit support among the more prosperous citizens, was above all

[1] Ibid. p. 148.

[2] *Briefwechsel zwischen Bruno und Edgar Bauer* (Charlottenburg, 1844) p. 163.

practical. It had the ideas of the Prussian Reform Era to look
back on and its philosopher was Kant. Radicalism was more
inspired by Rousseau and the French Revolution seen through the
eyes of the Young Hegelians and tended to be excessively theoretical. Liberal doctrines arose from the desire of the bourgeoisie
to be represented in the government, whereas radicalism was
limited to a small circle of intellectuals, who tended to adopt
revolutionary attitudes and reject compromises. The liberals, on
the other hand, had strictly limited aims, were in favour of reform
and wished to arrive at some sort of agreement with the monarchy.
Radicalism only made a definite appearance in 1841 when the
Young Hegelians began to turn their attention to political
questions. The tendencies then became more marked as can be
seen by comparing the radical *Rheinsiche Zeitung* with the liberal
paper of East Prussia, the *Königsberger Zeitung*. It was in the
Rheinische Zeitung that attacks on the idea of a middle road
appeared first. Edgar Bauer was the chief propagandist for this
view which saw only two irreconcilable parties warring against
each other. After the break with the Berlin Young Hegelians,
who evolved in the opposite direction, the term 'democracy' began
to replace the vaguer 'radicalism' in the *Jahrbücher* and the group
round Ruge, who were much influenced by Feuerbach. The anger
against the liberals was all the greater in that the Young Hegelians
considered themselves to have been abandoned by them in the
struggle with the government. Early in 1843 Ruge rejected
liberalism outright: 'the German world has to adopt the new way
of thinking which . . . makes free men the principle and the people
the object of its action, in other words it has to transform
liberalism into democracy'.[1] Later Ruge attributed the suppression of the *Deutsche Jahrbücher* to their criticising their own
liberal past, 'their theoretical love of liberty and their call to
transform liberalism into democratic theory'.[2] Ruge's concept of
democracy was still a very idealistic one, to be achieved merely by
propaganda. A conversation with Hess on this subject in 1843
shows that, unlike Hess, Ruge had no conception that 'even the
most radical political reforms are powerless against the root evil

[1] A. Ruge, 'Selbstkritik des Liberalismus' in *Deutsche Jahrbücher*,
2 January 1843.
[2] A. Ruge, *Sämtliche Werke*, VI, p. 84.

of society. The interest of each and all is in reality social reform '.[1]
But the acceptance of this transition was to cause yet another
split in the School.

h. Contemporary Influence of the Young Hegelians

Although the religious writings of the Young Hegelians, particularly those of Strauss and Bruno Bauer, had a profound and
lasting influence, in the political field their effect at the time was
very small indeed. Hegelianism as a whole was losing its hold in
Germany, especially after the accession of Frederick-William IV,
and the Young Hegelians never represented more than a small
part of the School. The universities were almost immediately
closed to them and the lectures that Bauer gave in Bonn were not
popular. Their only means of influencing opinion was through
their publications. It is true that the *Rheinische Zeitung* became
extremely popular just in the few months before its suppression
and that it increased its sales enormously, but the time was much
too short for it to make any impact. The *Hallische Jahrbücher*
certainly started with a wide following of contributors and at first
it was welcomed with great enthusiasm, being something completely novel on the German scene. F. T. Fischer wrote to Ruge
at the beginning of 1838: 'Your *Jahrbücher* is at present the most
read journal in the library, quite thumbed and worn'.[2] It seems
to have been read by people as far afield as Belinsky and Herzen.[3]
Delbrück, too, recalled that its influence at the beginning was
considerable, but that it subsequently declined owing to the
journal's radicalism. By the end of 1839 Ruge was complaining
about the trouble the journal caused him: not only did it make no
money, but both he and Echtermeyer had had to spend considerable sums on it and work without any remuneration. He wrote to
Feuerbach that the number of subscribers was only 313 (Köppen
referred to them as the 300 Spartans) and asked him to keep the
number a secret. Wigand the publisher hoped that the number

[1] A. Ruge, *Zwei Jahre in Paris*, i, p. 39.

[2] A. Ruge, *Briefwechsel*, i, p. 118.

[3] Cf. A. Koyré, *Études sur l'histoire de la pensée philosophique en Russie*
(Paris, 1950) p. 193.

would be over 500 by the following year and that in four or five years' time they would manage to cover the costs.[1] This hope, however, was not realised, and in 1842 the subscribers still numbered only about 500.[2]

i. Government Reaction

Undoubtedly the Young Hegelians would have become more radical, even if left to themselves, but the measures enforced against them at the end of 1842 made different forms of extremism inevitable. The government had already given signs of the forth-coming measures. Eichhorn had succeeded Altenstein as Minister of Culture and he was well known to be anti-Hegelian. Friedrich Julius Stahl, a jurist and leading supporter of an auto-cratic, hierarchical state, succeeded to the chair of the liberal Gans and, most obvious of all, in February 1841, Schelling was called to Berlin, in the words of the King to root out 'the dragon-seed of Hegelianism'. The inaugural lecture of Schelling's course on 'The Philosophy of Revelation' was given in November 1841 amid scenes of great enthusiasm and expectancy. Among those in the audience were Bakunin, Engels and Kierkegaard. The effect was by no means so dismal a failure as is usually alleged. Rosenkranz describes the Berlin philosophical scene in early 1842 in these words: 'Schelling and Schelling again this year. And he certainly deserves it. How a great man does stir everything up! Months and months have gone by and all the newspapers, journals and pamphlets are still full of things about him. Several Hegelians have started secret negotiations with Schelling. . . '.[3] The next step of the government was to deprive Bruno Bauer of his *licentia docendi*. Bauer had been sent to Bonn in 1839 by Altenstein to protect him from criticism in Berlin. But his writings became more and more radical while during 1840–42 he was working on his *magnum opus Kritik der Synoptiker*. With the death of Altenstein Bauer's hope of preferment disappeared and the question of whether he would be allowed to continue his

[1] L. Feuerbach, *Briefwechsel*, ed. Grün (Heidelberg, 1874) I, p. 298.
[2] Ibid. p. 354.
[3] K. Rosenkranz, *Aus einem Tagebuch* (Berlin, 1853) p. 107.

teaching dragged out a long time. Eichhorn, the new minister,
was actually quite restrained but was forced into taking a stand
when Bruno Bauer sent him personally the second volume of his
Kritik and demanded that all the theological faculties be con-
sulted as to its contents.   Eichhorn complied and the vast
majority of the faculties replied that Bauer's theories were incompatible with Christianity, but they were nevertheless against
his dismissal by sixteen to eleven.   But by that time Eichhorn
wanted no more bridge-building and revoked Bauer's *licentia
docendi* at the end of March 1842.   This decision was extremely
important not only as Bauer was the leading spokesman of the
Young Hegelians, but also as this was the first occasion that
Eichhorn was forced to declare himself *vis-à-vis* their doctrines
and it was obvious that in the future the universities would be
completely closed to them.

j. The Young Hegelians as a Political Party

It has been said that the Young Hegelians were the first political
party in Germany, and there is much truth in the statement. But
they only became a political party gradually and their party was
never exclusively political. They began, as has been shown, in
other fields, and only slowly concentrated on politics as the process of secularisation advanced.   Rosenkranz, describing this
process in 1843, said that 'the concept of a party has come over
into politics from the Church via literature and philosophical
schools.'[1]   Already by 1838 they were recognised as a party,
though not a political one, for Leo began each of the accusations
he formulated against them with the words 'this party'.[2]   By the
end of the 1830s political overtones had already entered in: for
Buhl, parties 'incorporated the dialectic' and could prevent
revolution, and Edgar Bauer in his articles in the *Rheinische
Zeitung* claimed that parties could control the hitherto chaotic
movements of the masses.   But unlike East Prussia, where the
party was viewed as a means of educating people to political life,
the Young Hegelian notion of the dialectic, as set forth in the

---

[1] K. Rosenkranz, *Über den Begriff der politischen Partei* (1843) p. 13.
[2] H. Leo, *Die Hegelingen* (Berlin, 1838) p. 2.

Rheinische Zeitung and the *Deutsche Jahrbücher*, tended to produce revolutionary oppositions. A political party represented a
principle and they were necessary for development.[1] The
emphasis was on their programme's being clear and on the need
for struggle. Their revolutionary character was aided by the
poets Herwegh and Hoffmann, with their enthusiastic paeans to
the party as 'artisan of victories'.

At the same time journalism, the only remaining means of
publicity, began to be endangered. The *Hallische Jahrbücher*
had become more and more extreme after 1840. Rosenkranz,
who did not approve of the change, wrote in his diary in 1842 that
he could already foresee its downfall: 'It is a great pity about this
journal, which began so excellently; but Ruge has let himself
succumb completely to radical tendencies. . . . The *Jahrbücher*
have come to the point where no contribution is accepted unless
it is written in a brusque, dictatorial, atheistic and republican
tone'.[2] Following some articles in February 1841 that directly
criticised the Prussian government, Ruge was ordered to publish
his review in Prussia and submit it to the Prussian censorship.
This he refused to do and so migrated to Dresden in Saxony and
changed the name of the review to *Deutsche Jahrbücher*. The range
of contributors also narrowed very considerably at this time.
Ruge saw them as consisting of three main parties: the more
traditional Hegelians, such as Rosenkranz; the group at Tübingen around Strauss and the aesthetician F. T. Fischer; and,
third, the atheists Bruno Bauer and Feuerbach. Soon Ruge found
it very difficult to pilot the *Jahrbücher* among such very varied
opinions: 'I am now in a bad way . . . the whole Prussian world is
deserting the *Jahrbücher*: Vatke, Schaller and their like. Their
culture and, in part, their learning is a loss that I feel greatly'.[3]
The Swabian theologians had already founded their own journal
in Tübingen disgusted with the over-violent attacks on Strauss,
and so Ruge was left with only the most extreme party. This
entailed a change in emphasis of the review – there were many
more articles dealing with philosophical problems and political
questions from a theoretical point of view and less on art and

---

[1] K. Marx, *Frühe Schriften*, I, p. 197.

[2] K. Rosenkranz, *Aus einem Tagebuch* (Berlin, 1853) p. 109.

[3] A. Ruge, *Briefwechsel*, I, p. 239.

literature. In April 1841 Feuerbach published his *Das Wesen des Christentums*, which affected Ruge very profoundly: he described it as 'the most noteworthy and important book of contemporary German philosophical writing'.[1] Feuerbach's influence in the *Jahrbücher* was definitely more marked from that date on. Ruge even began to attack liberalism and advocate democracy and republicanism, and in January 1843 the review was suppressed by the Saxon government at the instigation of Frederick-William IV.

Things went the same with the *Rheinische Zeitung*: the Young Hegelians had already given it the reputation of being a radical paper, and the correspondence of Hess from Paris contained accounts of communist doctrines. The paper was attacked by the *Augsburger Allgemeine Zeitung* for the propagation of communist doctrines, a charge which Marx, who in the autumn of 1842 was more and more closely associated with the editorship, emphatically denied. The circulation was still small but it mounted steadily. Earlier in the year there had been many contributions from the *Freien* in Berlin, but they quarrelled simultaneously with Ruge and the *Rheinische Zeitung*. Ruge had come to Berlin in November 1842 with Herwegh and the publisher Wigand to discuss the idea of founding a new university, but was shocked by the behaviour of the *Freien* whom he described as a 'frivolous clique'.[2] Ruge had also wanted to persuade them to moderate the tone of their writings so as not to compromise the common cause, but Bauer insisted to him that they had 'to pass beyond such concepts as state and religion and also property and family, without bothering to find a replacement, the essential thing being to deny everything'.[3] The cause of the break with Marx and the *Rheinische Zeitung* was essentially the same. Herwegh sent to the paper a letter in which he castigated the attitude of the *Freien* and Marx had it printed. He had already had difficulties with the contributions he received from Berlin, considering them too extreme and too abstract. He explained his difficulties as follows in a letter to Ruge: 'I permitted myself to cross out as much as the censor. For Meyen and Co. sent us heaps of scribblings written any old how, pregnant with world

[1] A. Ruge, *Zwei Jahre in Paris*, II, p. 57
[2] A. Ruge, *Briefwechsel*, p. 287
[3] Ibid.

revolution, empty of ideas and salted up with atheism and communism.'[1]

Marx was concerned with more practical matters, and demanded that if it were necessary to criticise religion it should be done within the framework of political institutions and not political institutions criticised within the framework of religion. Following the break with Berlin Marx contributed a very forthright and well-documented series of leading articles on the poverty of the Moselle vine-growers. This caused a worsening of the censorship and in January 1843, following protests of the Tsar at criticisms of Russian autocracy, the decision was taken to suppress the *Rheinische Zeitung* which ceased publication on the 31 March of that year. Already in December 1842 a series of similar measures had been taken which left the Young Hegelians without any means of propagating their views. In November Edgar Bauer's book defending his brother had been confiscated, on 18 December Buhl's journal *Der Patriot* was suppressed, on 27 December Herwegh was expelled from Prussia and the following day the liberal newspaper *Leipziger Allgemeine Zeitung* was forbidden in Prussia.

k. *Split in the Young Hegelian Movement*

These measures taken by the government against the radical press in 1842–3 led to an almost immediate fragmentation and dissolution of the Young Hegelian movement. Above all a movement of intellectuals, with no large-scale backing among the people and no interests in common to hold them together, they were doomed to disappear together with their organs of publicity. In the *Anekdota*, a two-volume collection of articles that had been rejected by the censorship and published in a book form by Ruge in March 1843, can be seen the different tendencies of the Young Hegelians movement united for the last time. The first volume was political: two articles by Ruge on the liberty of the press and Bruno Bauer's dismissal; Marx on the government's instruction relaxing the censorship. Bruno Bauer had two articles, Feuerbach was represented with his 'Vorläüfige Thesen zur Reform der Philosophie' and Ruge wrote a long and enthusiastic review of

[1] Marx, *MEGA*, I, i, 2, p. 285

Das Wesen des Christentums. Feuerbach's influence on the
Young Hegelians had reached its high point.

But the articles of the *Anekdota* already belonged to a struggle
that was past, and in the face of the government's measures the
movement split into two groups – the Berlin Young Hegelians
and those around Ruge. Those in Berlin expected a popular
reaction to the dismissal of Bruno Bauer and the suppression of
the radical press, and started a propaganda campaign that consisted of doctrines much more extreme than their previous ones
and an even greater insistence on the revolutionary power of
ideas. This tendency had begun in the middle of 1842 immediately after the dismissal of Bruno Bauer. For Bauer himself and
his Berlin friends his dismissal had a huge importance for they
thought that it would inaugurate the crisis leading to the hoped-
for revolution. It brought to a head all the debates of the time
and would help to resolve them. For the imminent catastrophe
that Bauer had written about in his letters was now at hand. He
immediately returned to Berlin to lead the struggle from there
and wrote to Ruge: 'If this affair is not exploited we shall not
easily get another one. I shall not rest until I have exploded all
the theological faculties. I shall do everything and try everything'.[1] He immediately brought out a book in his own defence
Die gute Sache der Freiheit, but it was his brother Edgar who
was the most prolific. He produced a defence of his brother
Bruno Bauer und seine Gegner and then a series of articles in the
Rheinische Zeitung in which he attacked all forms of compromise.
They showed very little political sense (which is why Marx broke
with the Bauers), believing, and saying, that those who were not
for them were against them. The liberal press had protested
strongly at Bauer's dismissal but nevertheless Edgar Bauer re-
served his most violent attacks not for the Prussian government,
but for the men of the centre, the *juste milieu,* and thus destroyed
any hope there might have been of getting popular opinion on their
side. Bruno Bauer even became tired of his Berlin friends who
were 'only very slightly coloured by the new principles'.[2] He

[1] B. Bauer, Letter to Ruge, 1 March 1842, unpublished. Photocopy
in International Institute for Social History, Amsterdam.

[2] B. Bauer, Letter to Ruge, 15 June 1842, unpublished. Photocopy
in International Institute for Social History, Amsterdam.

nevertheless continued to believe in the imminence of a very important crisis and in order to precipitate it published *Das entdeckte Christentum*, probably the most violent attack ever launched on Christianity, where his idea of religious alienation was expressed more forcibly than ever. And it was in this hectic atmosphere that Stirner began to collect the material for his book *Der Einzige und sein Eigentum*.

3. THE FOUNDING OF THE 'DEUTSCH-FRANZÖSISCHE JAHRBÜCHER' AND THE ORIGINS OF GERMAN SOCIALISM

a. The beginnings of the ' Deutsch-französische Jahrbücher'

Meanwhile Ruge, Hess and Marx wished to continue the struggle by founding some sort of review to replace the *Deutsche Jahrbücher*. The most obvious method was to use the publishing house of Julius Fröbel, professor of minerology at Zürich, whose radical views inclined him to publish anything that had been banned in Germany. The *Anekdota* had appeared there thanks to Fröbel as were to appear the future books of Bruno and Edgar Bauer. Fröbel had had plans to turn a small magazine of his own into a review capable of replacing the *Deutsche Jahrbücher*, and asked Herwegh to edit it, but Herwegh was expelled from Zürich and this brought the idea to an end: the articles already collected, including one by Bauer on the Jewish question and, more importantly, the articles by Hess on his philosophy of action and communism were published in book form under the title *21 Bogen aus der Schweiz*.

It was at this moment that the Young Hegelians began to think seriously about a collaboration with the French. Hess had already spoken often in favour of the idea that France and Germany were complementary and Feuerbach in his 'Thesen' had recently come out strongly in its favour. So Ruge and Marx conceived the idea of publishing a review entitled *Deutsch-französische Jahrbücher* at Strasbourg. This, however, proved impossible and Fröbel suggested either Brussels or Paris. This latter was agreed on and Ruge and Hess, who had agreed very readily to collaborate, fearing arrest in Germany, arrived there together early in August 1843. Ruge opened a subscription list of 1000 shares for the *Jahrbücher* but only ten were taken up and he had to contribute a considerable sum of money himself.

Among the future collaborators of the *Deutsch-französische Jahrbücher* there was very little unity of doctrine. Marx wrote in a letter to Ruge of September 1843, published later in the *Jahrbücher* 'If there is no doubt about the past and where we come from, there is great confusion when it comes to defining the goal to reach. Not only does a general anarchy reign among the reformers, but each has to admit to himself that he has no clear idea of what his programme ought to be'.[1] All of them, Hess, Bakunin, Ruge, Fröbel, Herwegh, Marx and Engels, considered themselves disciples of Feuerbach. They all accepted the necessity of doing away with alienation to arrive at humanism. The liberals had, they considered, abandoned the course of freedom and socialism was not yet a clear enough idea in their minds to present a viable alternative. Most of them, including Marx, would have been content to be described as radical democrats. The general vagueness of their ideas is clearly shown by the fact that at the end of 1843 the words humanism, democracy and communism were used almost interchangeably. Feuerbach had described his principles as 'egoism and humanism, since both are as inseparable as head and heart, without egoism no head, without communism no heart'.[2] Fröbel wrote in a letter to a Swiss communist: 'Greet Weitling from me and tell him that I do not yet know how far I can go along the communist path, but that meanwhile my heart is in the cause. I divide men into egoists and communists and, thus understood, I belong to the latter. The future will make the *how* plain, but I am in agreement as far as the *what* goes'.[3] Ruge also had no evil to say of communism at this stage and it was only later events that made him change his mind so forcefully.

[1] K. Marx, *Frühe Schriften*, i, p. 447.

[2] L. Feuerbach, *Sämtliche Werke*, ii, p. 391.

[3] J. Bluntschli, *Die Kommunisten in der Schweiz* (Zürich, 1843) pp. 63 f.

b. The Origins of Socialism in Germany

The socialist cause was not very far advanced in Germany at this time. At the end of the eighteenth century there had been one or two German writers who had propagated near-socialist ideas, but it was not until the 1830s that socialism began to have an appreciable effect on the intellectuals. The doctrines of Saint-Simon were propagated by the books of Heine and the lectures of Gans at Berlin that Marx followed assiduously. These ideas came in especially via South Germany and the Rhineland. In the latter, for example, Ludwig von Westphalen, Marx's father-in-law to whom he dedicated his dissertation, was a great admirer of Saint-Simon. Also in Trier at this time was Ludwig Gall who had given up his post as secretary to the town council to try to found a Fourierist phalanstery in America. It failed, but Gall returned to Trier and continued to preach Fourier's ideas on the increase of class division and to advocate the setting up of co-operatives. Nevertheless, the influence of these ideas was very small and confined to the intellectuals – indeed there were no socialist members at all in the German parliaments before 1848. Those like Georg Büchner or Weidig, who had tried to spread these ideas among the people, were harshly suppressed and it was only outside Germany that progress could be made. The first German workers' associations date from 1832 in Paris and a little later in Switzerland; here the most important figure was Wilhelm Weitling, who had produced his first book in 1838, *Die Menschheit wie sie ist und wie sie sein soll.* Weitling was a tailor by profession and his utopian communism and passionate rhetoric gave him a wide influence in these expatriate workers associations.

Inside Germany social questions did not come to the fore until after 1840. Ruge, writing an obituary of Echtermeyer in 1844, said that a work of Echtermeyer's on the romantic politicians had been definitely dated from the practical point of view by the 'critique of society and state that Anglo-French socialism offered and whose principles had already in 1842 aroused the attention of Germany'.[1] 1842 was the year of increasing government measures against those suspected of communist attitudes and also of the accusation of communism against the *Rheinische Zeitung.* Bruno

---

[1] A. Ruge, *Zwei Jahre in Paris*, 1, p. 152.

D

Bauer wrote later: 'At the beginning of 1843 communism had become such a widespread slogan that the *Literarische Zeitung* could describe the programme published by Ruge in the last number of the *Deutsche Jahrbücher* as a pale reflection of communism'.[1] In these years the words 'socialism' and 'communism' were used almost interchangeably by Hess, for example, though as time went on communism was regarded as a more militant, more revolutionary, less utopian brand of socialism. Among the Young Hegelians, the *Europäische Triarchie* of Hess, Heine's articles on Paris and the works of Feuerbach (it was the 'Vorläufige Thesen' and 'Grundsätze' much more than *Das Wesen des Christentums* that helped to focus attention on social problems) had prepared the ground, but the book that did most to bring socialism to the public eye in Germany was Lorenz von Stein's *Sozialismus und Kommunismus des heutigen Frankreichs*. Stein was a young, conservatively inclined academic, a Hegelian, who after finishing his studies in Berlin was given a scholarship by the Prussian government to go to Paris to study socialist and communist doctrines and to keep an eye on the activities of the German workers' associations there. In this summary of the results of his enquiry Stein presented socialism and communism as the logical consequence of the French Revolution. Industry meant competition and competition meant the reduction of salaries: thus the proletariat could never possess any private property. Stein helped to popularise the word 'proletariat' in Germany. It had first been used in German by Franz von Baader in contrasting the Bavarian 'proletariat' with the propertied classes. For Stein it was the needs of the proletariat and their social position that were the causes of communism, a view that Hess strongly criticised as 'materialistic', for the needs of the head and the heart were just as strong as those of the stomach. But for Stein reform could not remain at the political level but would have to deal also with the repartition of wealth. If the state did not take the initiative then this would mean a proletarian revolution. Stein condemned the doctrines he was describing and his book was conceived as an appeal to the ruling classes. He considered an enlightened and disinterested monarchy the best hope of reform. Nevertheless the book had a

[1] B. Bauer, *Vollständige Geschichte der Parteikämpfe in Deutschland* (Charlottenburg, 1847) III, p. 23.

wide influence among those interested in the new ideas because, as Karl Grün put it later, 'it constituted in some ways the first encyclopaedia of a new movement about which at most ten men were thinking in all Germany'.[1]

During the years immediately preceding 1848 the propagators of 'true socialism' did have quite a considerable following, particularly in the Rhineland and Westphalia, as is shown by the many newspapers and journals that spread their doctrines. However, those interested were still only the bourgeoisie. The conferences on communism organised by Hess and Engels in Wuppertal in 1845 met with a great success until suppressed by the police, but we learn that none of those attending came from the proletariat.

c. *The Failure of the 'Deutsch-französische Jahrbücher'*

To return to the *Deutsch-französische Jahrbücher*: once the financial basis of their review had been secured by Ruge, he and Marx began to look for contributors. They pressed Feuerbach very strongly to come in with them, but he refused considering that their political activism was premature. In order to clarify their ideas before approaching the French, Ruge, Marx, Bakunin and Feuerbach exchanged letters subsequently printed in the journal that reflected very well their doctrinal disarray. Ruge and Feuerbach were pessimistic on the chances of a revolution in Germany, Bakunin thought that revolution was the only answer, while Marx was quite unhopeful for the future, placing his confidence in a true democracy and criticising communism as being a 'dogmatic abstraction . . . itself only a particularly one-sided realisation of the socialist principle'.[2]

Ruge arrived in Paris with Hess in August 1843, filled with expectation. At the end of the journey, he wrote, 'we find the wide valley of Paris, the cradle of Europe, the great laboratory where world history is being elaborated. . .'. However, he was due for disappointment, the socialists to whom Hess introduced him being either indifferent or openly hostile. Almost without

[1] K. Grün, *Neue Anekdota* (Darmstadt, 1845) p. 123.
[2] K. Marx, *Frühe Schriften*, i, p. 448.

exception they were believers and held to Robespierre's anathema
of godless philosophy. Lamennais recommended them to associate themselves with one of the political parties and was shocked
at their opinion that science should be viewed as independent of
religion and man as the final end of the moral world. Louis Blanc
told them that their anti-religious propaganda was dangerous and
only helped the liberal bourgeoisie: they should declare themselves for socialism without making a detour via humanism.
Lamartine agreed at first to write an article for them but then
backed out as he thought the review too revolutionary. Proudhon
was not in Paris at the time, and Leroux had given up all intellectual work in order to perfect a new printing machine. Cabet
was shocked at their atheism, dismayed at there being no communist party in Germany and also at Ruge's unwillingness to call
himself communist. Finally Considérant, though sympathetic,
considered their position as too prone to violence.[1]

It quickly became evident that Ruge and Marx would have to
publish the review without French help, and even the Germans
were not numerous, although Heine, whose opinions had become
more radical since he had moved to Paris, did agree to collaborate.
In the end, the first and last number of the *Deutsch-französische
Jahrbücher* came out in March 1844 containing minor contributions from Ruge, Hess, Herwegh and Heine, Engels' article
'Umrisse zu einer Kritik der Nationalökonomie', which had a
great influence on Marx, together with a criticism of Carlyle, and
finally two articles by Marx 'Zur Judenfrage' and 'Einleitung
zur Kritik der Hegeleschen Rechtsphilosophie'. The first of these
criticised the liberal view of the state and the Rights of Man and
the second was a brilliant and forceful résumé of the German
radicals' views on religion, the political backwardness of Germany
and faith in the proletariat as a future emancipator of society.

Back in Berlin, the Young Hegelians had been zealous in
propagating their own ideas. Three currents can be discerned:
Bruno Bauer had just published his *Das entdeckte Christentum*,
and was waiting for his revolutionary ideas to have some impact.
Edgar Bauer brought out two books that were of more immediate
importance. In *Liberale Bestrebungen* he attacked the liberal

[1] On this series of visits, see Ruge's fascinating account of an
innocent in the Paris socialist *salons* in *Zwei Jahre in Paris*, I, pp. 69 ff.

movement in East Prussia and South-West Germany and insisted on an utterly radical opposition. In *Streit der Kritik mit
Kirche und Staat* he gave voice to ideas that were to become the
doctrines of Ruge and Marx: the egoistic institutions of the state
had private property as their basis and its abolition was necessary.
Thus the state would be dissolved into society and the class to
accomplish this transformation could only be those who had no
property. Thirdly there was Max Stirner whose book *Der
Einzige und sein Eigentum* was the culmination of Berlin Young
Hegelianism putting its faith neither in pure criticism nor in
democratic revolution but in the self as superior to all ideas and
things. Here Stirner was merely taking to their extreme the
doctrines advanced by the Bauer brothers in their journal that
they founded at the end of 1843 and which appeared for exactly
a year thereafter – the *Allgemeine Literatur-Zeitung*.

This review, which was something of a counterpart to the
Deutsch-französische Jahrbücher, was the last production of the
Young Hegelians. Its main theme was that, since the public had
accepted with indifference the suppression of the press and all the
illiberal measures of the Prussian government, the radicals had
been wrong to put their trust in the people, the 'mass', and that
in future criticism should hold aloof from all such deceptive
alliances. The enthusiasm of the masses was the worst obstacle
to progress in ideas. Every dogmatism, whether religious,
political or social, should be avoided so that criticism should be
completely pure and completely free. This meant, according to
Bruno Bauer, that 'criticism has ceased to be political. Whereas
before it opposed opinions to opinions, systems to systems and
views to views, it has now no opinion, no system, no view'.[1]
Ludwig Buhl founded about the same time the *Berliner Monatsschrift*, whose aim he defined in the first number: 'We do not
wish to replace one form of state with another and we have formed
no party, for our aim is solely to convince. Freed from any tie we
can, by means of purely theoretical position, claim the right to
research without hindrance and we hope, by isolating ourselves
from the parties, to escape persecution'.[2] However, this review
was still forbidden by the censorship, a fate which the review of

[1] B. Bauer, *Allgemeine Literatur-Zeitung*, VIII, p. 7.
[2] L. Buhl, *Berliner Monatsschrift*, pp. 2 ff.

the Bauer brothers escaped since the censors did not consider it at all dangerous. Although they lasted longer than the *Deutsch-französische Jahrbücher*, all the reviews of the Berlin Young Hegelians were dead by 1845 and, as was only to be expected, the movement that had thrived so much on the publication of journals ceased to exist.

The *Deutsch-französische Jahrbücher* ceased publication after a single double number. As has already been said, there were extreme divergences of view among the collaborators to the review. The material resources, too, were very unsure: copies were seized at the frontier into Prussia and warrants were issued for the arrest of Ruge, Marx, Heine and Bernays. Success in France was very limited and no doubt owing to the lack of French collaborators few reviews bothered even to allude to the *Jahrbücher*. Fröbel had already given Ruge 2000 francs to offset the cost of printing the review but then changed his mind and refused all further co-operation. Lack of money also aggravated the differences between Ruge and Hess. Hess had found himself without employment in Paris and so had asked Ruge for an advance on the articles he was to contribute to the *Jahrbücher*. Ruge had given it to him but took his furniture as security and even after Hess had been forced to return to Cologne because of lack of resources pressed him continually for the remaining 200 francs. Money difficulties also embittered Ruge's quarrel with Marx and Ruge even went as far as paying him with copies of the review.

d. *Marx's Break with Ruge and the End of the Young Hegelian Movement*

However, these difficulties were only secondary to the deep differences of outlook among the contributors. Ruge's contact with the Paris communists and their refusal to collaborate with his review, had led him to change his opinion of communism. He complained of the communists' inordinate attachment to money (they had probably tried to borrow off him once too often) and the vagueness of their plans for abolishing private property which seemed to him merely to involve a 'levelling down'.[1] During the

[1] A. Ruge, *Briefwechsel*, i, p. 324.

actual preparation of the review Ruge, the joint editor, played almost no part as he was ill. The result did not entirely please him: He recognised that the doctrinal articles were important, but thought them badly written, some being too rough and Marx's being too stylised and epigrammatic. The differences between Ruge and most of the contributors to the *Deutsch-französische Jahrbücher* were prefigured in a discussion that he and Hess had on their way to Paris. Ruge, in reporting this discussion,[1] shows that he himself put his faith in propaganda, education and democracy, whereas for Hess even the most radical political reforms were incapable of curing the fundamental evil of society and people were thus not interested in them. The one essential thing that interested them was social reform.

The immediate occasion of Marx's break with Ruge was the poet Herwegh. Much in the same way as he did with the Bauer brothers and the *Freien* in Berlin, Ruge had criticised Herwegh's dissolute way of life saying that it interfered with his poetic gifts. This annoyed Marx and he formally broke with Ruge by letter in May 1844. Even after this break, however, the differences between Marx and Ruge were not very evident. The origin of their divergence lay in their attitudes to Feuerbach. Ruge had come to appreciate Feuerbach at the time of the publication of *Das Wesen des Christentums*, whereas Marx was won to Feuerbach by the 'Vorläufige Thesen' and 'Grundsätze'. This meant that Ruge was most struck by Feuerbach's view that religious ideas were merely the ideals of a species-being that had never been realised on earth and thus were mirrored in an unreal other world, and this brought him to a sort of religion of politics that conserved many Hegelian traits – the human spirit pressing forward to its increasing manifestation in history. Marx, on the other hand, had been more impressed by the two later articles where criticism of Hegel was more explicit and materialism more definite.

Nevertheless, Ruge seems to have approved in general of Marx's articles in the *Deutsch-französische Jahrbücher* and only criticised them on stylistic grounds. About this time, too, Ruge wrote a short piece entitled *Der Mensch, eine Skizze* which showed remarkable similarities to Marx's ideas in the Paris MSS.[2] Ruge

[1] A. Ruge, *Zwei Jahre in Paris*, i, pp. 29 ff.

[2] The manuscripts written by Marx in Paris during the summer of

laid emphasis on the impossibility of conceiving man, or even the
family, as isolated units apart from society and defined man in
terms of his social relations. Work, for Ruge as for Marx, was
the social activity *par excellence* and it was through work that
man produced himself, an idea that both writers explicitly referred
back to Hegel. Ruge wrote: 'It is in work that man's world is
produced, "it is here that man is first seen as such", says Hegel.
He is right. Man's true essence is that he is his own product'.[1]
Work was the production of man by means of the production of
all the things that condition him.[2] The job of society therefore
was to ensure that everyone could find his own fulfilment and
freedom through his work.[3]

The individualistic approach – 'the private person who takes
his stand on his own guaranteed private property'[4] led to slavery.
'The masses become slaves to those who happen to be better
favoured and to blind chance'.[5] The fact that the worker's
energies were exploited by private persons meant that he was given
over to pure chance. Ruge's general conclusion was that 'Man's
activity and fulfilment depend on his work; the result of the
exploitation of man for an end that is not his own produces
slavery'.[6]

It is of course true that in spite of these similarities Ruge still
remained to a large extent an idealist: his ideal humanism was to
be achieved by the service of each to the whole, all would help
create the human essence. The most noticeable difference that
separated him from Marx was his view that the state, not the
present one but a reformed version, could be the instrument of
man's reunification and freedom. A very interesting document
in this connexion has been preserved by the poet Hoffmann von
Fallersleben. It was hurriedly dictated to him on 20 November
1843 by Ruge, who had just returned from Paris, in response to a
request for a summary of his views. Men, said Ruge, were to
be educated by and for the state. The community of all free men
was to be the only owner of property, so that no individual

1844, given the title *Ökonomisch-philosophische Manuskripte* by the editor
of the *MEGA* edition.

[1] A. Ruge, *Zwei Jahre in Paris*, ii, p. 364.

[2] Ibid. p. 367.   [3] Ibid. p. 372.   [4] Ibid. p. 367.

[5] Ibid. p. 368.   [6] Ibid. p. 373.

owners could get in the way of the community. Ruge thought that the state was already moving in this direction by abolishing privilege, by expropriation, military service, abolition of monasteries, and proscription of dangerous secret societies. All citizens would work for themselves in as far as they worked for the state, that is all citizens would be state officials. There would thus be no more service of one man by another, no more classes, no more poor.[1] Thus, in spite of Ruge's strong inclination at this time towards a sort of 'state socialism', the similarity of his views with those of Marx on man, society, work and exploitation is sufficient to justify his public minimisation of their differences. In July 1844, Börnstein, the proprietor of *Vorwärts*, a radical paper published in Paris twice weekly, invited Ruge in an open letter to explain the divergences between himself and Marx, particularly on the subject of the Rights of Man. Ruge, in his reply in early July, maintained that he was chiefly concerned with the principles of humanism whereas Marx concentrated on their application, but that there was no great difference between them and he finished by quoting with approval the end of Marx's article '*Zur Judenfrage*'.

But however true this may have been at the time of writing, an article by Ruge in the same paper three weeks later gave Marx the opportunity of a public break with him. This article was occasioned by the view of Louis Blanc's journal *La Réforme* that the weavers' revolt in Silesia (the same that gave rise to Heine's famous poem) had inspired the King of Prussia with such fear that he had felt compelled to promulgate an ordinance to combat pauperism and that important social reforms were to come. Ruge, on the contrary, maintained that fear was not the motive of the king's ordinance and that no era of social reform was to follow. Ruge's argument was that Prussia was so backward politically that the weavers' revolt could be nothing but a purely local event. Frederick-William's administrative measures and his appeal to people's generosity showed that he considered pauperism as a natural disaster to which it was right to respond with means appropriate to natural disasters. Owing to the political situation in Prussia a revolution would have no chance of success and only

[1] Cf. Hoffmann v. Fallersleben, *Mein Leben* (Hannover, 1868) IV, pp. 59 ff.

political organisation and education could suppress the real causes of poverty: 'a social revolution without a political soul, that is, one that is not organised from a general point of view, is impossible'.[1]

Marx, in his reply, also published in *Vorwärts*, maintained that the king's ordinance could only be seen in its proper perspective if the nature of pauperism were understood. Pauperism was not at all peculiar to Germany: it existed in England, too, and had as its cause the existence of private property. In England and France the bourgeois state had proved incapable of abolishing pauperism. It is thus plain that the abolition of pauperism is not dependent on the development of political reason. On the contrary: the more developed politically a country, the less are people likely to see the cause of pauperism in 'social' problems. The French Revolution is the typical political revolution: all that Robespierre saw in poverty and riches was an obstacle to the establishment of true democracy. Indeed political development is retrogressive since it obscures proletarian self-consciousness. The workers of Lyon thought of themselves as soldiers of the Republic pursuing political ends whereas in reality they were the soldiers of socialism.

Marx then went on to defend the German proletariat against Ruge's charge of backwardness. He praised Weitling very warmly and said that the Germans were the theoreticians of the European proletariat, just as the English were the leaders on the economic plane and the French politically.

This article caused a final break between Marx and Ruge, who also became estranged from Hess and even Bakunin. When Guizot ordered his expulsion from Paris in 1845 he settled in Zürich and began to edit his collected works, so losing contact with his former colleagues.

As soon as the *Deutsch-französische Jahrbücher* were published Marx had undertaken a vast course of study centred on the French Revolution. Ruge wrote in May to Feuerbach that 'Marx reads a lot. He works in an extraordinarily intensive fashion. . . . He finishes nothing, interrupts each line of research to plunge into a new ocean of books'.[2] It was quite natural that Marx, having proclaimed his faith in the proletarian revolution

[1] A. Ruge, *Vorwärts*, 2 July 1844.
[2] A. Ruge, *Briefwechsel*, I, p. 343.

as the emancipation of Germany, should take a close look at the last great example of revolution. He therefore abandoned his intention of writing a critique of Hegel's *Staatsrecht* and planned instead to write a history of the Convention. This undoubtedly did much to form Marx's view on the class struggle as did also his reading at the same time of the great French historians Thierry, Guizot, Mignet and Thiers. During the closing months of 1844 Marx turned his attention more to economic studies. The works of Weitling and Hess, to which he acknowledges his debt,[1] undoubtedly had an influence on him, but far the most important at this juncture was another Young Hegelian, Friedrich Engels, whose article in the *Deutsch-französische Jahrbücher* entitled 'Umrisse zu einer Kritik der Nationalökonomie' was more decisive than Engels' modesty would later allow him to claim. In it Engels had criticised capitalism for being irrational and inhuman. Engels argued that capitalism had produced a concentration of wealth in the hands of a few, divided mankind into two warring groups and by accentuating the struggle between the bourgeoisie and the proletariat made a communist revolution inevitable. Engels visited Marx in Paris at the end of August 1844 (though they had been exchanging letters since the publication of the *Deutsch-französische Jahrbücher*) on his way back to Germany from Manchester and they found that their views coincided so much that they decided on immediate collaboration and Marx began a study of the principal economists from Boisguilbert to Jean-Baptiste Say and James Mill. The hastily written and unco-ordinated fruit of these various areas of study may be seen in the Paris MSS. written towards the end of 1844, beginning with extracts from the classical economists, ending with a critique of Hegel's dialectic and having as their core sections on private property, the alienation of labour and money.

Marx attended the meetings of a society calling itself 'The League of the Just' and was very impressed by his encounters with the workers in Paris. In his Paris MSS. he wrote of them: 'fraternity among men is not for them a simple phrase, but the very expression of a reality, and all human nobility is reflected in these faces hardened by labour'.[2] However, Marx never actually

[1] K. Marx, *Frühe Schriften*, I, p. 507.
[2] Ibid. p. 618.

became a member of the League for he disapproved of their vague and syncretist mixture of French socialism and German philsophy. He no doubt thought, too, as did Engels, that secret societies were an obstacle to the organisation of a general workers' movement and moreover gave the government an excuse for oppressive measures. At the same time Marx became very friendly with Heine and when he had to leave Paris he wrote that Heine was the person he was most sorry to leave behind. Heine had been interested in social questions by Saint-Simon, but always had an ambivalent attitude to the proletarian revolution, his aristocratic leanings making him fear it as much in practice as he thought it inevitable and desirable in theory.

The first result of the collaboration of Marx and Engels was *Die heilige Familie* subtitled *Kritik der kritischen Kritik*,[1] a long polemic against the Berlin Young Hegelians and Bruno Bauer in particular. It might seem odd that, just at the time when Marx had freed himself from the influence of his former Young Hegelian colleagues and uncovered fields of enquiry that seemed to him to be more fruitful, he should spend time writing a large book of this kind. But it merely shows how much the scene was still dominated by philosophical arguments. Georg Jung, who regularly sent copies of Bauer's review, the *Allgemeine Literatur-Zeitung*, to Marx urged him to write a detailed criticism. The August number of the *Allgemeine Literatur-Zeitung* had contained an attack on communism as the 'mass' with which spirit was constantly in struggle. Marx had also announced in the Paris MSS. a general critique of Bauer's position.[2] Probably, too, there was something of the desire that prompted the writing of the *Deutsche Ideologie* 'to settle accounts with our former philosophical ideas'. The main reason, however, was a desire to attack and expose a position that Marx and Engels still thought was important: Bauer's Berlin circle of Young Hegelians was at this time the only radical voice in Germany and seen as the direct competitor of the Paris group. They need not have bothered, however, for before *Die heilige Familie* was published the journal of the Bauer

---

[1] That 'criticism' was still the order of the day is shown by the fact that one reply to Marx and Engels was entitled *Kritik der Kritik der kritischen Kritik*.

[2] K. Marx, *Frühe Schriften*, I, pp. 509f.

brothers had ceased publication and the *Freien* had ceased meeting. In January 1845 Marx was expelled from Paris by the Guizot government as a result of representations made by Prussia following criticisms of Frederick-William IV in *Vorwärts*. Thus by the end of 1844 the Young Hegelian movement was dead as a coherent force.

BRUNO BAUER

1. SKETCH OF BAUER'S LIFE AND WRITINGS

BRUNO BAUER and his two younger brothers Edgar and Egbert were descendants of Frankish farmers and their father had been a painter of porcelain. The family seems to have been fairly well off. There was a big house in Charlottenburg which the brothers used later for their publishing and Edgar speaks of an annuity left him by his grandfather.

Bruno Bauer had studied theology under Hegel for the three years immediately preceding the death of the Master and had, in 1829, on Hegel's recommendation, won the philosophical prize with a Latin essay entitled 'Uber das Prinzip nach der Kantischen Philosophie'. He was appointed lecturer in theology at Berlin in 1834 and first attracted attention during the discussion on the controversial book of D. F. Strauss *Das Leben Jesu*. Bauer was invited to review the book in the *Evangelische Kirchen-Zeitung*, which was edited by Hengstenberg, then professor of theology at Berlin and powerful head of the orthodox-pietist party. Strauss had denied the possibility of God revealing himself in a single individual: Jesus was for him only the imaginary representation of the incarnation of God in the whole human race. The Gospels were interpreted as the products of the messianic expectation of the early Christian communities. Bauer, in his review, tried to justify speculatively the historicity of the Gospels and in 1838 followed this up with a two-volume *Religion des Alten Testaments*, which was written from the same point of view.

Very soon, however, Bauer evolved more and more towards a radical form of criticism based on destroying religious beliefs rather than justifying them. This evolution concerned the object of criticism rather than the method. Whereas before criticism merely showed the deficiencies of past religious ideas and how they stood in contradiction with development towards the perfect harmony, now criticism began to demonstrate the absurdity of any kind of religion. Criticism became exterior as well as interior. In a piece of autobiography written in 1840 he described how the disciples had 'lived like the blessed gods with patriarchal calm in the realm of the idea' but that with Strauss's book 'the lightening of thought struck into the kingdom of the idea and disturbed the dream'.[1] He went on to describe how the critics of Berlin had put forward a reviewer of Strauss's book who 'still talked in the holiest of dreams of the unity of the idea and immediate reality or rather the world of empirical consciousness and was even bent on forwarding his dream in a special journal'.[2] This gradual evolution began in 1839 when Bauer threw down the gauntlet in a pamphlet attacking Hengstenberg designed to show that there was an unbridgeable gap between the Hegelian approach to the Bible and that of the orthodox party. As a consequence of this, Altenstein, the Minister of Culture, who was well disposed to the Hegelian School moved Bauer to Bonn in order to shield him from attack but here Bauer felt even more out of place and missed the society of his fellow Young Hegelians in Berlin. In 1840 he published *Die preussische Landeskirche* in which he claimed that by the union of the Calvinist and Lutheran Churches in 1817, the state church that resulted had forfeited the right to suppress criticism. Religion must henceforth not be something separate but immanent in the state, which was the ultimate seat of reason. With much self-questioning and inward struggle he arrived at a complete break with Christianity based on the conclusions he arrived at in his *Kritik des Johannes* (1840) and his *Kritik der Synoptiker* (1841–42). Bauer took the view that the evangelical records were not faithful records of historical fact. He did not give them all equal value, as Strauss tended to do, but went into minute investigations to determine their chronological order. These accounts, Bauer believed, reflected the mind of the individual evangelists, themselves only passing stages in humanity's self-consciousness. This passing stage had got fixed in institutional form and Bauer conceived his works as an exposé of the irrationality of Christianity when compared with the present stage

[1] B. Bauer, *Die evangelische Landeskirche Preussens und die Wissenschaft* (Leipzig, 1840) pp. 2f.

[2] Ibid. p. 3.

of self-consciousness. For Christianity, however revolutionary it was in its inception, had now been surpassed and become an obstacle to progress. This radical criticism, combined with the fact that Frederick-William IV had just succeeded to the throne and the new Minister of Culture, Eichhorn, was by no means as sympathetic to Hegelianism as his predecessor, combined to secure Bauer's dismissal from his post at Bonn. This event precipitated a crisis in the development of Bauer's thought and the Young Hegelian movement as a whole. Bauer immediately produced a pamphlet defending his position *vis-à-vis* the state, *Die gute Sache der Freiheit*, another on the relationship of religion to politics, *Die Judenfrage*, and finally one of the most bitter attacks ever to have been made on Christianity, *Das entdeckte Christentum*. Bauer was convinced that the revolution he conceived himself to have brought about on the intellectual plane would inaugurate one in practice too. When, however, he received little support for his cause and, at the end of 1842 and the beginning of 1843, the important radical papers were easily suppressed by the government, Bauer altered his outlook, decided that the time for revolution was not yet come and devoted himself to a criticism that had no immediate political ends. In 1844 he founded, with his brother Edgar Bauer, a review of his own, the *Allgemeine Literatur-Zeitung*, but it ceased publication after less than a year and Bauer's contributions to the Young Hegelian movement ceased with it. Although Bruno Bauer, unlike his brother Edgar, remained faithful to his beliefs about Christianity and continued his researches sometimes under the most difficult circumstances, politically he became in later years highly conservative and collaborated with Hermann Wagener, one of Bismarck's closest advisers.[1]

[1] It will be obvious from the above that Bauer's ideas undergo a development and it would be wrong to take quotations from any part of Bauer's writings as indicative of his thought in general. It is worth while mentioning here in particular the book of Sidney Hook *From Hegel to Marx* which is the only work in English dealing at any length with Bauer. Its whole treatment is vitiated by Hook's inability to view Bauer's writings in conjunction with the Young Hegelians as a political movement and in particular his inability to take account of the changes of outlook occasioned by the defeat of radicalism in 1842–3. Hook

2. BAUER AND HEGEL

The question of the relationship of Bauer's thought to that of
Hegel is one that has elicited very different answers. The most
recent to be published says that 'whoever has a deep knowledge
of Hegel recognises in Bauer a good disciple who in his own
beautifully styled and clear method turned the dialectic of his
Master to the better understanding of a historical period'.[1]
Gustav Mayer, also, whose long essay is still fundamental for the
understanding of the Young Hegelians, says 'Bauer handled the
Hegelian dialectic with virtuosity', and it was 'made for his type
of mind'.[2]

---

subtitled his book *Studies in the Intellectual Development of Karl Marx*,
but in reality what the book does is rather the opposite: Hook takes
the intellectual position that Marx had accepted by 1844 or 1845 and
contrasts with this position the various ideas of the Young Hegelians.
Especially is this the case with regard to Bruno Bauer. Marx's critique
of Bauer published in 1845 under the title of *Die heilige Familie* only
refers to Bauer's journal *Allgemeine Literatur-Zeitung* in which Bauer
specifically rejects the ideas of a philosophy of action and of revolution
that he had advocated, however idealistically, in the years 1841–3.
In as far as this is the case, Marx's remarks, which serve as a guide to
those of Hook – and Marx is a notoriously bad guide to his opponents'
views – have no relevance for the period under discussion. In addition,
it is obvious that Marx in *Die heilige Familie* is only concerned to
emphasise the points that divided him from Bauer, not their common
ground. However, not only does Hook fail to take into account the
earlier period of Bauer's writings, he also confuses it with the period of
'pure criticism'. For example, under the heading 'Terrorism of
Reason', which refers to Bauer's revolutionary criticism, Hook quotes
a passage (not even written by Bauer, as Hook alleges, but by his
disciple Szeliga) from the *Allgemeine Literatur-Zeitung* of 1844, ideas that
Bauer would certainly have disowned earlier. Quite apart from whether
the attack of Marx on Bauer in *Die heilige Familie* is justified, the
important point is that Marx is dealing with Bauer's views at the time
of writing, that is those of the so-called 'pure criticism' of 1844, and
taken those as representative of Bauer's whole development, as Bauer
himself complained later, thereby leaving out of discussion Bauer's
writings 1840–3 which are far more important and influential.

[1] G. A. van den Bergh van Eysinga, in *Annali*, IV, (Milan, 1964)
p. 346.   [2] G. Mayer in *Zeitschrift für Politik* (1913) p. 46.

E

This view, however, is profoundly mistaken. In many respects, certainly, Bauer was faithful to the spirit of his Master: the central concept of his philosophy – that of 'self-consciousness' – comes from Hegel's *Phänomenologie*. Hegel, too, had offered philosophical interpretations of Christian dogmas and portrayed historical situations as provisional and bearing within themselves the elements of future changes. Where Bauer radically parted from Hegel was in his conception of the dialectic. Hegel's dialectic is certainly an obscure affair and its clarification has unfortunately not been proportionate to the amount of discussion devoted to it; but there are still some points about it that can be clearly made. The dialectic is a process and at the same time a progress, that is, it leads from one state of affairs to another which is higher or more complete. Yet the latter does not exclude the former, which still remains part of it. The word that Hegel uses to describe this transition is *aufheben* which he himself explains as follows: 'Aufheben has in the German language a double meaning in that it signifies conserving, *preserving* and at the same time also making cease, *making an end*. Even conserving includes the negative aspect that something is taken out of its immediacy and thus out of an existence that is open to external influence, to be preserved'.[1] Bauer, however, changed the dialectic into a purely negative one: instead of the later state of affairs being the expression of former one-sided ones in their completion, it now negated them and was, in extreme cases, their exact opposite. This version of the dialectic became more and more accentuated in the Young Hegelian movement until it found its classic expression in Bakunin's article 'Die Reaktion in Deutschland', published in the *Deutsche Jahrbücher* in 1842 under the pseudonym of Jules Elysard. This shift in emphasis was inevitable in one who admired as much as Bauer did the *Aufklärung* and the French Revolution, whose atmosphere Bauer tried to reflect in his writings with considerable success. Ruge called him the 'Robespierre of theology'[2] and Cieszkowski referred to his 'scientific terrorism'.[3] Bauer certainly had reservations about the writers of the *Aufklärung* – deism was still in the background, they did not realise

[1] G. Hegel, *Werke* (Berlin, 1832ff.) iii, pp. 110f.
[2] A. Ruge, *Briefwechsel*, i, p. 281.
[3] A. von Cieszkowski, *Gott und Palingenesie* (Berlin, 1842) p. 97.

that religion was a historical phenomenon, like all creations of the human spirit, and they conceived of men as being too determined by nature – but the *Aufklärung* had 'solved the problems of religion and humanity in general'[1] and, though his language was thoroughly Hegelian, Bauer drew much of the inspiration for his incisive arguments and crusading spirit from the eighteenth century.

There is also a second way in which Bauer's version of the dialectic diverges from that of Hegel. Whereas Hegel had tried very hard to preserve a unity between thought and being, Bauer, and the Young Hegelians in general, gave the precedence to thought, that of the human subject. There only remained the subjective side of Hegel's philosophy of identity.

The *locus classicus* for the Young Hegelian view of Hegel, and a small masterpiece of their particular style of writing, is Bauer's pamphlet *Die Posaune des Jungsten Gerichts über Hegel den Atheisten und Antichristen*, where he endeavours to show that his own view is really that of the Master's too. It is also a highly amusing piece of writing, the (anonymous) author posing as an orthodox pietist and feigning to warn his co-religionists not only against the Young Hegelians, but also against Hegel himself. The text itself is extremely striking as all sorts of different printing techniques and even fingers pointing to various passages were used to give the words maximum emphasis. The pamphlet was subtitled *Ein Ultimatum* and that was what it was: an attempt to demonstrate to all opponents the exact nature of the Hegelian philosophy. Bauer develops the idea of an 'exoteric' and 'esoteric' Hegel, the difference between what Hegel said or appeared to say and the true nature of his system. It was true, said Bauer, that there was a difference between the Young and the Old Hegelians, but 'in the final analysis, if we go back to the teaching of the Master, the later disciples have invented nothing new: rather they have removed the cloak with which the Master covered his assertions and revealed the system in all its nakedness'.[2] Hegel makes much talk of God and the unity of philosophy and

[1] B. Bauer, 'Die Fähigkeit der heutigen Juden und Christen frei uz werden', in 21 *Bogen aus der Schweiz*, ed. G. Herwegh (Zürich and Wintherthur, 1843) II, p. 62.

[2] B. Bauer, *Posaune*, p. 149.

religion, but this should deceive no one: Strauss developed it into
a sort of pantheism, but even more dangerous was what was plain
to anyone who wished to examine closely: 'the concept of religion
according to which it is only a relationship of self-consciousness to
itself'.[1] Hegel's great achievement in this field had been that
he had done his best to reconcile philosophy and religion, but
without success. The theologians and religious people had raised
a great outcry about 'pantheism', but the Hegelians did not pay
them any heed until all paths towards the reconciliation had been
tried and found wanting. Now it had been shown that philosophy
and religion were incompatible and it had to be admitted that
Hegel's system was pantheism and even more.[2] What Bauer set
out to demonstrate was how Hegel himself dissolved the idea of
religion and how infinite self-consciousness was the only thing
that remained. In the political field, too, the essence of Hegel's
philosophy was held to be equally radical. His theories are
described as 'revolution itself' and himself as 'a greater revolutionary than all his disciples put together'.[3]

Ruge was a great admirer of the *Posaune* and called it a book
of world-historical importance, 'a necessary break with all the old
tradition of Hegelianism'.[4] Feuerbach, however, saw more
accurately when he objected to the *Posaune*'s being ascribed to
himself, saying that the *Posaune* was *for* Hegel, while he was
against him.[5]

In other writings of the same period Bauer arrives at the same
result, but modifies somewhat his judgement of Hegel by in-
corporating elements that have a very Fichtean tone: it is true
that Hegel sometimes speaks of self-consciousness as conditioned
by substance – that is matter separated from mind – but his system
itself corrects this point of view. His own principles perforce
raise substance to the free creation and ever-renewed product of
self-consciousness. If Hegel seemed occasionally to give too much

[1] Ibid. p. 151.
[2] Cf. *Anekdota zur neuesten deutschen Philosophie und Publizistik*, ed.
Arnold Ruge (Zürich and Winterthur, 1843) II, p. 131.
[3] B. Bauer, *Posaune*, p. 171.
[4] L. Feuerbach, *Briefwechsel und Nachlass*, ed. K. Grün (Leipzig and
Heidelberg, 1874) I, p. 337.
[5] Ibid. p. 330.

importance to the recognition of substance, this was only because he wishes to counterbalance the empty ego of rationalism. However (and this was where Bauer's interpretation differed a little from that in the *Posaune*) Hegel himself was not fully aware of the consequences of his own system. 'It is precisely the arguments of the last few years', says Bauer, 'that have brought about the fulfilment of the Hegelian system.' Hegel tried to separate certain principles and powers from man's self-consciousness, but now criticism had shown that self-consciousness embraced everything, and being the sole power of the universe draws everything into its orbit. The conclusion, however, was the same, and it was the 'genuine' Hegel who was claimed to have taught the Young Hegelians 'atheism, revolution and republicanism'.

It is not important to decide how far this is a true representation of Hegel's ideas: the answer is probably that it is far from accurate. For, when dealing with religion, Bauer only took into account Hegel's historical critique of religion and not his higher integration of it before absolute knowledge at the end of the *Phänomenologie*. Moreover, in Hegel's sketch of the progress of man's spirit, Bauer's self-consciousness, being highly subjective (Hegel would have classed it as a master-type and thus incapable of development), comes before even the 'unhappy consciousness'. But it was never Bauer's intention to give an accurate exegesis of the Hegelian text. His aim was rather to point out those aspects of Hegel's thought that were important for the future. And undoubtedly his interpretation of the dialectic was accepted throughout Young Hegelian circles.

3. BAUER AND CHRISTIANITY

Bauer's view of Christianity may be roughly summed up like this: since history represents the dialectical progress of humanity's self-consciousness, and Christianity appeared at a certain moment in the past, it cannot be its final product. Certainly human self-consciousness took a step forward with Christianity, but since it submitted mankind to an arbitrary God and dogmas that he himself has unconsciously created and since mankind is now becoming conscious of its independence, Christianity is at present

the most serious obstacle to universal self-consciousness. Bauer
submits the texts of the Gospels to a very close examination to
discover the contradictions in them and to prove that they were
free compositions of individual creative minds. He also shows
how the world situation in the early Roman Empire favoured the
rise of Christianity and then gives a general characterisation of it.

How did the Gospels come into existence? Bauer maintained
that there was an individual personality behind each one of them.
But the evangelist did not merely write down what was given him:
he was its creator. Christianity owed its origin to the genius of
the original evangelist who wrote St. Mark. This Gospel was a
work of art created by its author. Bauer maintained that the fact
that a piece of writing was also a work of art not only influenced
the content but created it. The community was only aware of the
life, death and resurrection of Christ. They wanted more details
and the evangelist supplied them and interpreted through these
details the spirit of his age.

What was, according to Bauer, the situation of the world at this
time that was so favourable to Christianity? Bauer showed himself a true disciple of Hegel in that, for his explanation of the
Gospels, he concentrated precisely on that period of thought to
which Hegel in his *Phänomenologie* had assigned 'self-consciousness' – the post-aristotelian Greek thinkers. Indeed, the
whole of Bauer's work in this field was, as Marx remarked,[1] a
commentary on Hegel's 'Unhappy Conciousness'. They were,
according to Bauer, the true basis of Christianity. Their
individualism prepared the way for the universal domination of
Christianity by loosing men from all social ties as the world of the
city was breaking up. The Roman world had already established
the principle of individuality. The Emperor concentrated all
rights and interests in his own person and there was nothing left
to link together the individual citizens. The people lost confidence in themselves and doubted their ability to enjoy a valid
political life. Viewed in this context, Bauer described Christianity
as 'the religious expression of this unbelief . . . and the dissolution
of political and civil relationships into their magic reflections.'[2]
It is 'an expression of the disgust that antiquity felt against

[1] *MEGA*, i, i, 2, p. 308.
[2] B. Bauer, *Die Judenfrage*, p. 47.

itself'[1] and again 'the fright caused to antiquity by the disappear-
ance of its political institutions, its art and science'.[2]

The universal domination of Rome and the impact of Greek
philosophy could not liberate man properly because religion had
still a great influence on human consciousness: so the revolution
had to take place inside a religious context. In this still alienated
sphere previous limits were done away with and the religious
alienation could become total. The following vivid quotation
gives a good idea of Bauer's view: with the appearance of
Christianity

> the ego was everything and yet it was empty; it had become the
> universal power, yet, still among the troubles of the world, it
> was afraid of itself and doubt assailed it because of what it had
> left behind. The empty and all-embracing ego was fearful of
> itself, it did not dare to conceive of itself as everything and the
> universal power, that is it remained a religious conception and
> completed its alienation in that it placed its own universal
> power over against itself and worked in the sight of this power
> in fear and trembling for its preservation and holiness. It saw
> the guarantee for its support in the Messiah who merely repre-
> sented what it itself was in reality, that is the universal power,
> but the universal power that it was itself, one in which all
> feeling for nature, all ties of family race or state, all forms of art
> had disappeared'.[3]

Bauer's attitude towards Christianity is thus ambivalent. On
the one hand, it was a necessary stage in human development, yet
it was to be deplored and condemned. On the other hand, it
represented an advance and progress *vis-à-vis* previous religions,
yet it was at the same time the worst religion. The necessity of
Christianity Bauer explained as follows:

> These contradictions [that is, of Christianity], however un-
> natural they may seem, are still not unnatural; however much
> they contradict man's essence, they are nevertheless a conse-
> quence of it. They are contradictions against man himself, but
> it lies in the nature and vocation of man that in his historical

[1] B. Bauer, *Christentum*, p. 141.
[2] Ibid. p. 143.
[3] B. Bauer, *Synoptiker*, iii, p. 310.

development he enter into contradiction with himself and bring
this contradiction to a culmination before he can attain to
harmony with himself.[1]

Christianity, as well as being necessary, is also in one way a
genuine progress. For the religions of antiquity had as their
powers nature, the family and the spirit of genius of the people.
In Christianity mankind freed itself from this attachment to
nature. Judaism had indeed preceded Christianity here, by
expressing the dependence of the world on human consciousness
in its belief that God created the world. Christianity adopted a
more human approach, though still in a religious form, by seeing
the essence of man in all things.

But if Christianity was universal and did not know the limits of
previous religions, it was at the same time the worst religion:
'Christianity is the religion that promised men most, that is all,
and took back most, that is all'.[2] Bauer attempts to explain this
ambivalence of Christianity thus: the nearer that religious consciousness approaches to truth, the more it alienates itself therefrom. Why? Because, qua religious, it takes the truth that is
only to be attained to in self-consciousness away from self-
consciousness and places it against self-consciousness, as though
it were something alien to it. What is opposed to self-consciousness as alien is not only formally separate from self-consciousness
(in that it stands outside it, is in heaven or comprises the content
of some long past or far in the future events), but also this formal
separation is backed up by an essential and real separation from
all that goes to make up human nature. When religion has
reached the point that man makes up its content, then the climax
of this opposition has been reached. In antiquity the extent of
the religious alienation was still hidden and Bauer has a touching
description of this type of religion:

The sight of nature fascinates, the family tie has a sweet
enchantment and patriotism gives the religious spirit a fiery
devotion to the powers that it reveres. The chains that the

[1] B. Bauer, *Das entdeckte Christentum*, p. 138.
[2] B. Bauer, 'Die Fähigkeit der heutigen Juden und Christen frei zu
werden', in *21 Bogen aus der Schweiz*, ed. G. Herwegh (Zürich and
Winterthur, 1843) p. 69.

human spirit bore in the service of these religions were decked with flowers and man brought himself as a victim to the religious powers festooned in an admirably decorative way. His very chains helped to deceive him about the harshness of his service.[1]

But in Christianity, by contrast, the freedom of the children of God was also freedom from all important worldly interests, from all art and science, etc. It was an inhuman freedom, in which what was only gained and kept through the use and development of the powers of the spirit disappeared. It was a freedom presented as a gift to be received with unconditional subjection. This freedom was therefore unlimited slavery under an authority against which there was no possibility of appeal. Thus in Christianity the alienation had become total, and it was this total alienation that was the biggest obstacle to the progress of self-consciousness.

4. SELF-CONSCIOUSNESS AND CRITICISM

The philosophy of self-consciousness played a central role in the ideas of the Berlin Young Hegelians from 1840 onwards. It rested on the idea of Hegel that consciousness, via a series of mediations arrived at a realisation of its position within the totality of thought. But Bauer was not content with Hegel's solution. The ego of Fichte and the substance of Spinoza were, according to him, still not reconciled, and it was obscure whether, in the final analysis, man or the absolute was the real motor of history. In general, Bauer decided in favour of the former, though sometimes he speaks of self-consciousness as though it were a force separate from the minds of men.

The essence of Bauer's concept of self-consciousness is *development*: as soon as self-consciousness has realised itself in one form, in one substance, this becomes a barrier to further development and must be supplanted by a higher form. Thus, for example, to attain to self-consciousness in the sphere of religion would be to come to realise that religious objects are really created by human

[1] B. Bauer, *Synoptiker*, III, p. 309.

subjects. Self-consciousness is aiming at ever greater and greater
universality; in the end the barriers that were holding up the
development of self-consciousness will fall and what was divided
will become united. Truth is the development of self-consciousness, self-consciousness in its universality. All that is necessary
is to create the circumstances in which it can advance freely, and
these circumstances have been well prepared by recent philosophical developments. Bauer regards his philosophy of self-
consciousness, somewhat paradoxically, as 'the truth of materialism', meaning that materialism has finally destroyed the domination of religion over men's minds and thus prepared the way for
self-consciousness, which Spinoza referred to obscurely as 'substance', to be all in all. There is thus no longer any point in
asking: What is self-consciousness for? What does it achieve?
For it is the source of everything, creates and destroys, consists in
its own movement and finds its aim and identity in this movement
alone. It is, to borrow another expression of Spinoza's, the true
causa sui.[1]

This extremely intangible notion, referred to once by Marheineke as 'a Pandora's box from which everything possible has
been extracted',[2] is made a little clearer by considering the means
through which self-consciousness was to be attained – criticism,
a word which was the constant battle-cry of the Young Hegelian
movement. Criticism is the activity that transforms objects into
self-consciousness. For self-consciousness and its progress em-
brace everything, because self-consciousness represents the unity
and power of the universe. Its object is to do away with all
obstacles that impede the progress of history. But criticism will
not always be negative: 'Up till now history has brought forth
no truth that has not fallen to the fire of criticism, but the highest
truth that she can now produce – through criticism – man,
freedom, self-consciousness, is the least calculated to block
criticism and future progress since it is nothing but development
at last freed'.[3] Neither is criticism purely subjective, its progress

[1] Cf. B. Bauer, *Das entdeckte Christentum*, pp. 160f.

[2] P. Marheineke, *Einleitung in die öffentlichen Vorlesungen über die
Bedeutung der Hegelschen Philosophie in der christlichen Theologie* (Berlin,
1842) p. 37.

[3] B. Bauer, *Die Judenfrage*, p. 81.

is not interior to itself but is dependent on its general situation. Bauer gives his most specific account of what he understands by criticism in the introduction to the *Kritik der Synoptiker*. Progress beyond a certain position 'must be made via knowledge and a sublimation of the starting-point and justified by the inner nature of the letter itself if it is to be a true progress, and what is this mediation apart from criticism? Does not criticism lead to self-consciousness in that it recognises in the latter, in the positive, a facet of self-consciousness?'[1] On the one hand, criticism is the last achievement of a particular philosophy which must thus free itself from a positive aspect that still limits its generality, on the other hand, it is the presupposition without which it could not raise itself to the final generality of self-consciousness. History, says Bauer, does not come towards us; our own action must bring us towards it. That action is called criticism.

It is important not to confuse this idea of the function of criticism with that adopted by Bauer after the failure of the radical movement in 1842–3. The phrase of M. Rubel – 'the pure intellectual activity of an areopagus of predestined thinkers'[2] – may well characterise Bauer's attitude in 1844, but it certainly does not represent his intention in the preceding years. He wrote, summarising what according to him was Hegel's position: 'The religious relationship is merely an inner relationship of self-consciousness to itself and all those powers which seem to be separate from self-consciousness, whether as substance or as absolute idea, are merely phases in self-consciousness objectified by the religious imagination'.[3] Thus Bauer, his philosophy *was* one of revolution. But since history was the process of self-consciousness and self-consciousness was formed by criticism, this led him to overvalue the importance of his own intellectual position and suppose that results would follow simply from the impact produced by his pamphlets. His view was that of the young Hegel: 'Once the kingdom of ideas is revolutionised, reality cannot hold out'.[4] For criticism is the action of applying theory to

---

[1] B. Bauer, *Synoptiker*, pp. xxf.

[2] M. Rubel, *Karl Marx, Essai de biographie intellectuelle*, Paris, 1957, p. 92.

[3] B. Bauer, *Posaune*, p. 151.

[4] *Briefe von und an Hegel*, ed. Hoffmeister (Hamburg, 1952ff.) I, p. 253.

reality as it exists, the critical negation of what exists. It is what
Bauer in a letter to Marx called the 'terrorism of pure theory'
whose job it was to 'clear the ground'.[1] This criticism is not
purely negative. Sometimes, it is true, Bauer sounds simply
destructive, as when he writes to Edgar: 'I have fully completed
criticism and freed it from any positive element',[2] but in other
passages this negation only appears as a preliminary. Nevertheless, an important question is: what sort of a revolution did
Bauer wish to see happen and how did he conceive of his work
affecting it? Did he really think, as a quick reading of some of his
articles and pamphlets suggests, that ideas could create a revolution or change anything that mattered? Was not Marx then
justified in saying that this demand to change men's consciousness merely amounted to a demand to interpret reality differently
and thus really to accept it?[3] Two preliminary points should be
made: Bauer's subject matter sometimes compelled him to be
rather far removed from reality for he was chiefly concerned in
attacking a very other-worldly Lutheranism; secondly, the style
of his writings, rhetorical articles, full of over-sharp antitheses and
written to make a swift impression, certainly seems to later readers
rather shrill and exaggerated. But if these points are taken into
account, Bauer appears as no mere dreamer, no believer in the
omnipotence of ideas. He was concerned with man, his essence
and his happiness. The very idea of alienation involves having a
clear picture of what is essential to being a man. Bauer's references to nature, too, show that he did not neglect material reality.
One of the reasons for his condemning Christianity was its 'un-
naturalness' and in *Das entdeckte Christentum* he followed Hol
bach in laying emphasis on arguments from evidence of the senses
and the laws of nature. He shows sympathy for the 'natural'
religions that preceded Christianity for their bringing out what is
characteristically human in man as an objective, material being.
Bauer was also a close observer of historical development, as one
would expect from his careful studies of early Christianity. For
him the movement of man's self-consciousness was what gave

[1] *MEGA*, i, i, 2, p. 247.
[2] *Briefwechsel zwischen Bruno Bauer und Edgar Bauer* (Charlottenburg, 1844) p. 133.
[3] Cf. Marx–Engels, *Werke*, iii, p. 2.

history its content and meaning. History was the journey on which men's minds became enslaved to their own creations and gradually, through an antithetical development, set aside these false idols and attained to unimpeded self-realisation. Thus for Bauer criticism could never be an end in itself – it had to be linked to the present needs of mankind, and that meant sooner or later becoming practical: 'action is inevitable, as is practical opposition and that not only as an afterthought or in a round-about way. No, a theoretical principle must straightaway become a practical act . . . the overthrow of what exists must be the main aim – so philosophy must also work in the political field and . . . attack existing situations'.[1] Bauer certainly recognised that history was not equivalent to the history of ideas: he seems to have thought that it had a movement of its own closely connected to, but not dependent on, the course of men's ideas. The exact relation he never made precise, but he certainly lacked Marx's optimism about the establishment of rational material conditions changing, at least in time, men's irrational ideas. Ideas, for Bauer, had a force of their own and were worth combating on their own. Indeed a victory in this sphere would be vindicated by history:

> We wish to complete our theory so as to prepare once for all a new path for history.[2] Theory, which has helped us so much remains even now our one hope of making ourselves and others free. History, which we do not control and whose decisive turns lie outside our reckoning, will . . . raise the freedom that theory has given us to a power that will give the world a new form'.[3]

Thus Bauer considered theory to be the strongest form of practice: it was only when the bourgeoisie had failed to respond to his ideas that he took a more detached view.

[1] B. Bauer, *Posaune*, pp. 82f.
[2] B. Bauer, *Die gute Sache der Freiheit und meine eigene Angelegenheit* (Zürich and Winterthur, 1842) p. 209.
[3] Ibid. p. 224.

5. ALIENATION

The third and most important concept of Bauer that requires close examination is that of *alienation*. Being by training a theologian, the alienation with which he is concerned is the religious one. This arises from a split in man's consciousness and the illusion that not only is there something existing apart from and independent of man's consciousness, but that he himself is dependent on his own creation. This division between man's consciousness and the object that it has created becomes more and more pronounced and the tension so unbearable that a final catastrophe produces a complete unity.

Religion is, according to Bauer, a division in consciousness where religious beliefs become opposed to consciousness as a separate power. Self-consciousness makes itself into an object, an imaginary separate being, a thing – an early formulation of the idea of reification. In this situation, self-consciousness loses control of itself, having deprived itself of all its value, and feels itself as nothing before the opposing power. A religious conscious-ness cannot exist without this breaking up or tearing apart of consciousness: it deprives man of his own attributes and places them in a heavenly world. In short, religion can be described as an attitude towards the essence of self-consciousness that has been alienated from itself. Bauer was the originator of the expres-sion 'self-alienation' that soon became current among the Young Hegelians.

While recognising that this alienation was in some way neces-sary and grounded in human nature, Bauer did not believe (as did Feuerbach) that religious beliefs were merely a *projection* of the human essence so that what was required was simply that man should reclaim for himself the objects that he has created: the alienation does not admit of such a simple 'reduction'. The very fact that these heavenly objects and ideas have their origin in a consciousness that is religious means that they are themselves misshapen and broken, unlike, for example, a work of art, a product on the purely human level, that is harmonious. Rather, since it is the work of a divided mind and the objectification of this very division, it stands in contradiction to itself. This explains why the Gospels are in contradiction with each other and the world and why later dogmas should be so far removed from common sense as to be only able to be understood as mysteries. In his last and most violent attack on Christianity Bauer put the point very forcibly by saying that the God men worshipped was their own imaginary, inflated and distorted reflection. God might have been created by man, but he was a *subhuman* God.

In this conception of alienation the choice is not simply between two well-defined poles – God or man – as Feuerbach had suggested. Bauer's view is much more subtle and macabre. Since man's condition is a twisted one, so are his ideas, his wishes, his God. A mere 'reduction' of the one to the other would do nothing to cure the evil: nothing short of a revolution in man's self-consciousness could achieve that.

But the condition of alienation is not a static one. Humanity cannot lose itself entirely; in worldly pursuits it still retains freedom and religious consciousness is forced to change through its connexion with this free consciousness. Humanity cannot be completely suppressed and strives all the time to gain its autonomy over against religion. At the same time, religion, to fulfil its vocation and nature, must become more and more estranged from self-consciousness, take no account of it and turn itself completely towards the other world. At the Reformation, Catholicism was simply declared to be a deception, but the true source of religion, illusion, the self-deception of servile people, remained. Indeed, in Protestantism, the illusion is complete and all-powerful: it envelops men not from the outside, but from the inside. In Protestantism, the feeling of dependence has reached its apogee: for where religion is conceived to be the essence of man, there he will find it most difficult to grasp his own true essence. Strangely, Bauer thinks that this other-worldly conception of religion is carried to its furthest in the rationalist conception of God. But since the alienation is total, this means that now at last a total liberation is possible. Bauer thus divides world history into two parts: the first, that of alienation and lack of freedom, and the second, which begins in the present time, the complete restoration of man for which previous history has been merely a preparation. The turning-point of history is the present age and the imminence of total liberation makes the character of the times 'catastrophic'. Bauer says in a letter to Marx: 'the catastrophe will be frightful, it will of necessity be a great one, and I would almost go as far as to say that it will be greater and more monstrous than that which accompanied Christianity's entrance on the world scene'.[1] Thus what the present age witnesses is the final battle with the 'last enemy of mankind . . . the unman, the spiritual irony of mankind, the inhumanity that man has committed against himself, the sin that it is most difficult of all to admit to'.[2]

This sin is 'the most difficult of all to admit to' since, although man cannot really avoid seeing that religious beliefs are his own work, 'just when he is about to look on them with human eyes, he shuts his eyes and flings himself down in adoration before his own work'.[3] The only thing that now prevents his complete liberation is the fear that man must lose himself before he completely wins himself back again, the fear that his essence will somehow escape him if he recognises it in God.[4] Nevertheless, Bauer believes that the critical vanguard, led by himself, has brought about the definitive demise of religion. Criticism has 'restored man to himself' and the religious question is 'eliminated for all time'. It only remains to publicise the fact sufficiently.

6. BAUER'S VIEW OF THE STATE

Bauer held a conception of the state that was completely in the Hegelian tradition. It was inside the framework of the state that man was to be united to himself. The state, created by self-consciousness, was 'the manifestation of freedom'.[5] Instrumental in Bauer's dismissal from Bonn was the toast he proposed at a Berlin banquet in honour of Welcker, the liberal statesman from Baden, a toast to Hegel's conception of the state which 'in

[1] *MEGA*, I, i. 2, p. 241.

[2] B. Bauer, *Die gute Sache der Freiheit* (Zürich and Winterthur, 1842) p. 185.

[3] Ibid. p. 17.

[4] Cf. ibid.

[5] B. Bauer, 'Der christliche Staat', in *Hallische Jahrbücher* (1841) p. 537.

its boldness, incisiveness and liberalism went far beyond the views predominant in South Germany'.[1]

This view, however, was called in question by the accession of Frederick-William IV. The king was fundamentally a romantic, and this meant that he saw a revelation of the divine principle in the Church alone and wished to subject the state to her. Bauer, however, as indicated, held a radically different view of Christianity, particularly where the state was concerned. Quite apart from the fact that Christianity belonged to a stage in the development of thought that had now become obsolete and thus could only impede future progress, it was also linked in Bauer's mind with the atomised sort of civil society that had been so well characterised by Hegel, and also by Bauer himself at the beginning of his essay on 'Die Judenfrage': 'Need is the powerful motor of civil society. Every person uses other people for the satisfaction of his own want .... Civil society is kept in being by need and creates the perpetual oscillation between riches and poverty, need and affluence'.[2] This type of society had as its principle Christianity, the religion of individual self-interest, egoism and complete subjectivity. The bourgeois constitutional state is the political expression of the essence of religion in the final stage of its ascendancy. Bauer opposes Christianity because it separates men from each other and their true essence: his aim is integration and the recovery of man's universal essence. It may cause confusion that Bauer in *Die Judenfrage* strongly supports the idea of natural rights which were really (as Marx pointed out) the expression of the very type of society to which Marx was opposed. The answer is that Bauer is using the language of the Enlightenment to clothe the ideas of Hegel. Natural rights, in the way in which Bauer uses the idea, do not delimit an area in which a man can act as he pleases; they are privileges that can only be attained to when all prejudices that might separate men from one another have been done away with.

Thus the consternation of Bauer and the Young Hegelians in general may be imagined when, contrary to their hopes, they realised that the principle that was opposed to all they

[1] *Briefwechsel zwischen Bruno Bauer und Edgar Bauer* (Charlottenburg, 1844) p. 163.

[2] B. Bauer, *Die Judenfrage*, p. 8.

F

wished a state to be was going to be given complete dominance.

Throughout the time that he was at Bonn Bauer tried to combat through his writings the result that he so much feared. The object of his attack was the 'Christian state'. This is the state in which the religious element either is, or is intended to be, the leading one. All state matters are pervaded by the influence of Church dogma: Byzantium is the supreme example of this. Bauer tries to show that throughout history religion, claiming that its role is boundless since divine, has tried to enslave the other powers of man's mind. The aim of the state is unity and harmony, whereas the Church divides man from himself. How then, if religion is to become the dominant force, can man hope to recover from his confusion? Bauer goes further and describes the Church as 'the alienated essence of the state'[1]: the Church was necessary to the state as long as it was not in a position to be the 'manifestation of freedom'. For, as religion is the objectified immaturity of man, so the Church is the practical expression of the imperfection of the imperfect state which does not have the courage to stand on its own feet.

Thus, although of course with time Bauer's views became more extreme – and Edgar went as far as rejecting any form of constitutional state – yet at first Bauer looked to the sovereign to create the sort of state that he would like to see. In *Die preussische Landeskirche* (1840) he appeals to Frederick-William IV saying that the people await from the throne the sign for the next turn that history will take. The state, he says, echoing Hegel, is the highest manifestation of freedom and humanity,[2] and the prince is the personal representation and existence of the sovereign power of the state.[3] Bauer ends his work with the words: 'If the state rejects us, yet we do not reject the state, but hold fast to the principle of the state as the highest there is. The final analysis will show that we have chosen the better part'.[4]

When the state seems to be adopting a policy contrary to his

[1] B. Bauer, *Die gute Sache der Freiheit* (Zürich and Winterthur, 1842) p. 40.

[2] B. Bauer, *Die evangelische Landeskirche Preußens und die Wissenschaft* (Leipzig, 1840) p. 97.

[3] Ibid. p. 100.

[4] Ibid. pp. 135f.

desires, he evolves a theory of opposition within the framework
of the state: 'In the dialectical flow of its future, the state is
never identical with a particular government so long as self-
consciousness has not yet been incorporated into the state'.[1]
The state, in other words, can be criticised without its existence
being called into question. But what exactly a state would look
like into which self-consciousness had been incorporated is not
very clear from Bauer's writings. What Bauer wants is 'the
general recognition by men of the essence that they hold in common'.[2] To this end the state must allow free enquiry and research
into all fields. All men must participate in political affairs.
Bauer sees no necessary contradiction between the general and
the individual interest. He praised the French thinkers of the
eighteenth century for their emphasis on self-love. The general
interest of mankind is my interest and their aims my aims. Man
cannot do without the community. If Bauer was not anxious to
describe closely his idea of the future (an inclination which all the
disciples had inherited from the Master) he was nevertheless sure
of the means to achieve it: 'Theory . . . has now completed its
part and can await with confidence the verdict of history'.[3]

7. BAUER'S INFLUENCE ON MARX'S DISSERTATION

Unfortunately, throughout the years of his close friendship with
Bruno Bauer, nothing has survived of Marx's writings with the
exception of his dissertation with which he gained the title of
doctor in April 1841. So, that apart, the nature of their relationship from 1838–42 has to be ascertained from other sources.
Luckily the series of letters that Bauer wrote to Marx during this
period has survived and shows how close their collaboration was.
Marx's period of study of religion and philosophy corresponds

[1] B. Bauer, 'Der christliche Staat', in *Hallische Jahrbücher* (1841)
p. 553.
[2] B. Bauer, *Die Judenfrage*, p. 19.
[3] Ibid. p. 115.

precisely to the period of his friendship with Bruno Bauer and was no doubt inspired by him. Also there was Bauer's dominant position among the Young Hegelians. He was a member of the Graduates Club that Marx joined immediately on his arrival in Berlin and was no doubt prominent in its discussions. Even when Bauer was in Bonn he returned to Charlottenburg for his vacations. Hess goes as far as to say of him that 'he stood at the head of the Young Hegelians'[1] and certainly his *Kritik der Synoptiker* gave him the leading position, especially in Berlin.

In 1842, the crisis year of the Young Hegelians, Cieszkowski said that 'if one wanted to say that Bruno Bauer was not an important philosophical phenomenon, then this would be like asserting that the Reformation was not an important event . . . Bruno Bauer *shines* on the horizon of knowledge: it is no longer possible to darken him'.[2] Ruge, too, valued Bruno Bauer greatly and made his views the centre of the *Hallische Jahrbücher* for 1841.

The influence that Bauer could be expected to exert on Marx from his position is borne out by what little we know of Marx's activities at this time. Marx, as we know from his university record, was not a very assiduous attender at lectures, and in 1839 Bauer's was the only one that he did not give up. Bauer was certainly very keen to see Marx in Bonn and wrote to him: 'Make sure that you get your wretched exam behind you and can devote yourself completely to your studies of logic'.[3] It was through Bauer that Marx hoped to obtain a post at the University of Bonn and Bauer even went so far as to give him advice about lectures: 'If you had not wished to lecture on Hermesianism[4] here next winter, then I would have chosen the subject for myself. But it is self-evident: you must lecture on the subject, if only because you have been studying it for so long'.[5] Later, however, the situation changed and Bauer advised against the subject as

---

[1] M. Hess, *Philosophische und sozialistische Schriften* (Berlin, 1961) p. 381.

[2] A. Cieszkowski, *Gott und Palingenesie* (Berlin, 1842) p. 93.

[3] *MEGA*, I, i. 2, p. 234.

[4] So called after Hermes, a professor at the University of Bonn, who had attempted a synthesis of Catholic dogma and Kantian philosophy condemned in 1835 by Rome.

[5] *MEGA*, I, i. 2, pp. 239f.

one for lectures. We also learn from Bauer's letters to Marx that the latter was engaged on a critical review of a book by K. P. Fischer called *Die Idee der Gottheit* and also on a critique of Hegel's *Religionsphilosophie*, the text of which Bauer was revising at that time for a new edition by his master, Marheineke. Both these works, neither of which has survived, seem to have been inspired by Bauer who also had a plan for editing in company with Marx a journal whose tendency is sufficiently shown by its title *Archiv des Atheismus*. In a 'profile' of Marx, written in 1843, the *Mannheimer Abendzeitung* said: 'Marx is a friend of Bruno Bauer with whom he wished formerly at Bonn to edit a philosophico-theological review which was to be based on Bauer's views in his *Kritik der Synoptiker*'.[1]

Nothing came of this plan and instead in October 1841 the *Posaune* appeared. It is very unlikely that Marx contributed to this in a direct way, but his association with Bauer was close enough for some to have thought so. Jung wrote to Ruge: 'Have you read the *Posaune* against Hegel? If you do not yet know, I can tell you, as a secret, that it is by Bauer and Marx'.[2]

Since their association was so close it is not surprising that Marx's only work of size to have survived from this period, his dissertation, is marked by many of Bauer's ideas. Bauer certainly gave Marx his advice on it and was against an open proclamation of atheism in the introduction. Marx did not take this advice, but nevertheless showed himself a disciple of Bauer when he wrote in the same introduction that philosophy was against 'all gods in heaven and earth that do not recognise human self-consciousness as the highest godhead. There shall be no other beside it'.[3]

There seems little doubt that the subject of Marx's dissertation – a comparison between the natural philosophy of Epicurus and Democritus – was inspired by Bauer. It is true that in the introduction Marx mentions the book of his friend Köppen, *Friedrich der Grosse und seine Widersacher*, saying that it contains a deeper treatment of the relation of post-aristotelian system to Greek life. But Köppen's book was only published in 1840 when the dissertation must have been largely completed. It has been said

[1] *Mannheimer Abendzeitung*, 28 February 1843.

[2] *MEGA*, i, i. 2, p. 262.

[3] K. Marx, *Frühe Schriften*, i, pp. 21f.

that Marx chose this subject since he found himself in the same position *vis-à-vis* the 'total' philosophy of Hegel as the Greek thinkers did after the 'total' philosophy of Aristotle. But there is no evidence for this; certainly Marx himself never said so. His attention was no doubt directed to this period by Bauer, as this was the period allotted by Hegel in his *Phänomenologie* to self-consciousness, and the point of his dissertation, according to Marx, was to solve a hitherto insoluble problem in the history of Greek philosophy and to emphasise the importance for Greek philosophy of these systems that Hegel had in general rightly characterised although the bold and large plan of his history of philosophy prevented him from going into the details.[1]

There is no reason to suppose any great influence of Feuerbach on Marx at this early stage. Had this been so, we would expect Marx to talk of 'man' instead of 'self-consciousness' and to bring in some typically Feuerbachian concepts, such as that of 'species' (*Gattung*). Marx's section on 'Reason and the Existence of God', where, if anywhere, Feuerbach's influence would be expected to show, still reads like an echo of Bauer: 'The proofs for the existence of God are nothing but proofs for the existence of essential human self-consciousness, logical explications of it. For instance, the ontological proof. What being is immediately given as soon as it is thought of? Human self-consciousness'.[2] Marx nowhere mentions Feuerbach, and Ruge's allusion in a letter to Feuerbach's joining the review that Bauer and Marx planned to found about this time must be mistaken, for Bauer in a letter to Marx writes in a way that suggests that Marx objected to Feuerbach's taking part.

There is a strong temptation to read back into the dissertation some of the later doctrines of Marx. There are, indeed, passages of vivid writing, but they contain no ideas that are peculiar to Marx: for example, when he castigates those who want to patch up the present philosophical situation with half measures 'whereas Themistocles, when Athens was threatened with destruction, persuaded the Athenians completely to desert their city and found a new Athens on the sea, a new element',[3] this is precisely

---

[1] Cf. ibid. pp. 20f.

[2] Ibid. pp. 75f.

[3] Ibid. p. 104.

the sort of apocalyptic idea that is so frequent in Bauer's writings. Bauer's doctrine of the value of pure negation comes to the fore in the passage where Marx claims that 'it is a psychological law, that the theoretical spirit that has become free turns into a practical form of energy and coming forth from the shadow kingdom of Amenthes in the form of will turns against worldly reality that is exterior and separate from it'.[1] Their attitude to Hegel is also very similar. Bauer's distinction in the *Posaune* between an esoteric and exoteric Hegel is repeated by Marx: 'If a philosopher has in reality compromised himself, then his disciples have to explain from his inner and essential thoughts what had for himself an exoteric form'.[2] Finally, Marx's view of the relation of theory and practice is precisely the same as Bauer's. His claim in the dissertation that 'the practice of philosophy is itself theoretical'[3] is taken from one of Bauer's letters to him that says: 'Theory is now the strongest form of practice'.[4]

In short, there is nothing at all in Marx's dissertation that shows him to be other than an ordinary Young Hegelian with a close sympathy for some of Bauer's ideas.

8. MARX'S BREAK WITH THE 'FREIEN'

Marx and Bauer drifted apart after Bauer's dismissal from his post at Bonn and Marx's collaboration and subsequent editorship of the *Rheinische Zeitung*. But to speak in these circumstances of a 'break' between the two is misleading. It is true that Marx broke with the Berlin group that called themselves 'Free Thinkers' but to suppose that this involved a break with Bauer is to misunderstand Bauer's relation to the group. This group was one based on the former Graduates Club that Marx had joined when he first came to Berlin and they called themselves 'Free Thinkers' to mark their more radical standpoint. They attained a certain

---

[1] Ibid. p. 71.
[2] Ibid. p. 70.
[3] Ibid. p. 71.
[4] *MEGA*, I, i. 2, p. 250.

renown when the *Königsberger Zeitung* published an article on their free-thinking ideas, but they were never of any great importance. They wrote articles for the *Rheinische Zeitung* and acted as its Berlin correspondents, but their point of view was too extreme and Marx was compelled by the position of his paper to steer a middle course. He objected to their extremely doctrinaire attitude and lack of concrete analysis, also to their advocacy of communism. In a long letter to Ruge explaining the causes of the quarrel he said:

> I declared that I considered that to introduce, as contraband as it were, socialist and communist ideas, that is a new conception of the world, into incidental theatre reviews was indecent and even immoral, and I asked them that, if they had to speak of communism, they would approach the question in a totally different and more profound manner'.[1]

When the 'Free Thinkers' did not qualify their extremism, Marx took the occasion of their quarrel with Herwegh to make his break with them public by publishing Herwegh's letter with its attack on them.

Bauer was not, however, a member of the Berlin group: he was still in Bonn when it was founded. So far from thinking that Bauer was in agreement with the standpoint of the 'Free Thinkers', Marx actually hoped that he would be able to modify them: 'It is lucky', he wrote to Ruge, 'that Bauer is in Berlin. At least he will prevent them from doing anything stupid'.[2] Bauer's own opinion of the group may be gauged from a letter of his to Ruge where he says that there is not much to be done with these 'Beer–literati, but one cannot desert them when one is living inside the same walls. Berlin is so poor that they are the only ones who have even been tinged by the new principles. Of course it remains the merest tinge and nothing more'.[3] How far Bauer was associated with the group is uncertain, but we possess a letter of his to Marx where he loyally stands by them, at the same time defends himself against the charge of belonging to a clique and

[1] *MEGA*, i, i. 2, p. 286.

[2] *MEGA*, i, i. 2, p. 278.

[3] B. Bauer to A. Ruge, 15 June 1842, unpublished letter. Original: International Institute for Social History, Amsterdam.

says he proposes to let bygones be bygones. Certainly he conserved his influence on Hess after this dispute, for Hess's articles
well on into 1843 are marked by Bauer's subjective idealism, and
there is no reason for thinking that it should have been any
different with Marx. Marx went so far in December 1842 as to
write a small article in defence of Bauer objecting to his dismissal
and he certainly continued to read his works with admiration.
In a letter to Ruge he praised Bauer's review of a book by Ammon
published in Ruge's *Anekdota* and he described *Die gute Sache der
Freiheit* as the best thing Bauer ever wrote.

9. BAUER AND MARX ON THE JEWISH QUESTION

During 1843 Marx first took open position against some of the
doctrines of Bauer. The beginning of this process can be seen
very clearly at work in the manuscript of Marx's *Kritik des
Hegelschen Staatsrechts*, written in the middle of 1843, where
Marx in several places crosses out the term 'self-consciousness'
which he had originally written and substitutes another term
more evocative of practical realities.

In his review essay 'Zur Judenfrage', published in 1844 in the
Deutsche-französische Jahrbücher, Marx explained precisely what
he disagreed with in Bauer's views. Bauer's position is admirably
summed up by Marx:

> he requires on the one hand that the Jew renounce his Judaism
> and, in a general manner, that man renounce religion in order to
> be emancipated 'civically'. On the other hand, as a logical
> consequence, he considers that the 'political' suppression of
> religion is equivalent to the suppression of all religion. The
> state that presupposes religion is not a true and real state'.[1]

Marx is also in favour of abolishing religious ideas. But, unlike
Bauer, he believes that the secularisation of the state is not
sufficient to achieve this nor is it sufficient to free man from his
real servitude. For the root of this servitude is not religious
alienation but political alienation: 'We do not see in religion the

[1] K. Marx, *Frühe Schriften*, I, p. 455.

foundation, but only the manifestation of secular deficiencies'.[1]

But Marx was very far from being in total disagreement with Bauer. He agreed with a large part of Bauer's thesis, and at the beginning of his article paid him this compliment: 'Bauer analyses the religious opposition between Judaism and Christianity and explains the essence of the Christian state; and does all this with dash, clarity, wit and profundity, in a style which is as precise as it is pithy and vigorous'.[2] What Marx admired and took over from Bauer's view of the Christian state was firstly his picture of present civil society as one of atomised individuals with no communal link and secondly the association of this with the 'egoistic' influence of Christianity. For the first, Bauer expresses himself at the beginning of the *Judenfrage* as follows

> Need is the powerful drive that sets civil society in motion. Each man uses the other to satisfy his own needs, and is again used by him for the same purpose.... It is precisely this foundation, need, which, while it ensures for civil society its existence and its necessity, yet exposes it to constant dangers, preserves within it an unsure element and produces the constant oscillation between poverty and riches, destitution and superfluity.[3]

Bauer's second point was that ultimately Christianity was responsible for this egoism, in that, as he says in *Das entdeckte Christentum*, it 'shuts off man from the great social interests of the world ... from art and science, it destroys his social being, his social customs, and inter-human links, it makes him single and isolated, an egoist, and brings about the sacrifice of all human aims and ends'.[4] Marx takes up both these points in a passage at the end of his essay:

> Civil society only reaches its perfection in the Christian world. Only under the sway of Christianity which objectifies all national, natural, moral and theoretical relationships, could civil society separate itself completely from the life of the state, sever all the species-bonds of man, establish egoism and selfish

[1] Ibid. p. 457.
[2] Ibid. pp. 452f.
[3] B. Bauer, *Die Judenfrage*, p. 8.
[4] B. Bauer, *Christentum*, p. 112.

need in their place and dissolve the human world into a world of atomistic antagonistic individuals.[1]

These similarities show that Bauer was by no means as abstract and content with merely religious criticism as a superficial reading of Marx would suggest. The above quotations are sufficient to show that Bauer, too, thought that a political emancipation would be necessary in addition to a religious one. At the very end of his essay he even went so far as to do, with as much clarity as Marx ever achieved, precisely what Marx criticised him for omitting: he explains 'The religious servitude of citizens by their secular servitude' and 'transforms theological questions into secular ones'.[2] Bauer's comment here is so strikingly akin to Marx that it deserves a long quotation.

[In the Middle Ages] religious prejudice was at the same time a prejudice for their corporations, religious privilege was only the supernatural conformation of civil privilege and religious exclusion only the presupposition, model and ideal of civil and political exclusion. Men have never done anything historical merely for the sake of religion. They have undertaken no crusades, they have waged no wars. When they imagined that they were acting and suffering for the sake of God, we can now not only affirm in the light of our modern insight into 'the things of God' that these actions and sufferings were much more about what man had to be and become, but we can also say that in all religious development, undertakings, struggles, tragedies and campaigns ... it was always political interests or their echoes ... that governed mankind. We would be understanding religious history falsely, that is as it understands itself, if we wished to think that it was only concerned with the divine and other-worldly. This other-world is rather the self-alienated world of men's interests projected into another world, the shape of this world is only an imagination of the order prevailing in human society, and its heresies and struggles only an attempt to bring the understanding of worldly interests into this imaginary world in a violent and inverted manner.[3]

[1] K. Marx, *Frühe Schriften*, i, p. 486.

[2] Ibid. p. 458.

[3] B. Bauer, *Die Judenfrage*, p. 114.

10. Bauer and the 'Einleitung zur Kritik der Hegelschen Rechtsphilosophie'

It is evident that while Marx was writing this article, where his idea of the development of history and the forces that control it first took shape, he had the writings of Bauer much in mind. It is a very striking fact that almost all the metaphors in the first two brilliant pages where Marx summarises his views on religion are borrowed from Bauer who is still his first and foremost model in this field.

Marx's remark that 'man who has found in the fantastic reality of heaven, where he sought a supernatural being, only his own reflection, will no longer be tempted to find the semblance of himself – a non-human being – where he seeks and must seek his true reality'[1] recalls Bauer's description of religion as an 'imaginary reflection'[2] and his idea of God as 'non-human' or even 'sub-human'.[3] When Marx calls religion the 'moral sanction of this world'[4] he is echoing Bauer's phrase about Christianity as 'the sanction of the imperfection of present circumstances'.[5] Bauer, too, says that religion is the 'expression' of these circumstances, and Marx follows this in saying that religious misery is 'the expression of human misery'.[6] The famous metaphor of the opium of the people was also anticipated by Bauer in his book *Die gute Sache der Freiheit* where he talks of how religion 'in the opium-like stupefaction of its destructive urge, speaks of a future life where all shall be made new',[7] and again in *Der christliche Staat* of the 'opium-like influence'[8] of theology on mankind,

[1] K. Marx, *Frühe Schriften*, i, p. 488.

[2] B. Bauer, 'Die Fähigkeit der heutigen Juden und Christen frei zu werden', in *21 Bogen aus der Schweiz*, ed. G. Herwegh (Zürich and Winterthur, 1843) p. 68.

[3] B. Bauer, *Christentum*, p. 156.

[4] K. Marx, op. cit. p. 488.

[5] B. Bauer, *Die gute Sache der Freiheit* (Zürich and Winterthur, 1842) p. 217.

[6] K. Marx, *Frühe Schriften*, i, p. 488.

[7] B. Bauer, *Die gute Sache der Freiheit* (Zürich and Winterthur, 1842) p. 213.

[8] B. Bauer, 'Der christliche Staat', in *Hallische Jahrbücher* (1841) p. 538.

though the expression was used by many of the Young Hegelians
who may well have taken it from Hegel's description of Indian
religion.[1] The image of the flowers on the chain – 'criticism has
plucked the imaginary flowers from the chain, not in order that
man shall bear the chain without caprice or consolation, but so
that he shall cast off the chain and pluck the living flower'[2] was
used by Bauer, who may have taken it from Rousseau, at the end
of his *Kritik der Synoptiker*. 'The chains that man bore in the
service of these religions (that is religions of nature) were wound
round with flowers ... his chains themselves deceived him concerning the harshness of his service'.[3] Marx's image of the
'illusory sun about which man revolved as long as he does not
revolve around himself'[4] is also drawn from Bauer, who used it to
indicate how near and yet how far Christianity was from expressing
man's true nature: Christianity's 'nearness to the sun is also its
furthest distance therefrom'.[5] Finally Marx proclaimed that with
the assistance of philosophy 'criticism of theology transformed
itself into a criticism of politics'.[6] This transition had already
been begun by Bauer in such essays as *Der christliche Staat* and
indeed Herwegh said of Bauer in 1843 in this connexion that all
theory was now turning into practice. 'Theology has, through
Bauer, for example, become politics'.[7]

Here Bauer's influence on Marx is very clear. He was by training a theologian and it was his criticism of religion that was of
primary importance for Marx, who adopted it entirely and – this
is the essential point – applied the same method of criticism to
other and, as he thought, more essential fields. The first words of
the *Einleitung* are: 'For Germany, the criticism of religion has
been largely completed; and the criticism of religion is the premise
of all criticism'.[8] This means that the various alienations are like

---

[1] Cf. E. Benz, 'Hegels Religionsphilosophie und die Linkshegelianer'
in *Zeitschrift für Religions- und Geistesgeschichte* (1955).
[2] K. Marx, op. cit. p. 489.
[3] B. Bauer, *Kritik der Synoptiker*, iii, p. 309.
[4] K. Marx, op. cit. p. 489.
[5] B. Bauer, Review of D. F. Strauss, 'Die christliche Glaubenslehre'
in *Deutsche Jahrbücher* (1843) p. 87.   [6] K. Marx, op. cit. p. 489.
[7] Quoted in V. Fleury, *Le Poète Georges Herwegh* (Paris, 1911) p. 336.
[8] K. Marx, *Frühe Schriften*, i, p. 488.

skins around the genuine centre. They have to be peeled off one
after another and it is only when the outside one has been peeled
away that the others are laid bare. The outer and most extreme
alienation is that of religion and the criticism of this leads to the
criticism of other alienations that must be dealt with in the same
way. In this way, the influence of Bauer follows Marx through
all his later criticism.

The effect Bauer had can best be shown in Marx's own words
when he criticised both the wings of the Young Hegelians; of the
wing led by Feuerbach (though Marx does not name him), which
he calls the 'practical party', he says:

> It supposes that it can achieve the negation of philosophy by
> turning its back on it, looking elsewhere and murmuring a few
> trite and ill-humoured phrases. Because of its narrow outlook
> it does not take account of philosophy as part of *German* reality,
> and even regards philosophy as beneath the level of German
> practical life and its theories. You demand as a point of
> departure real germs of life, but you forget that so far the real
> germ of life of the German nation has sprouted only in its
> cranium. In short, you cannot abolish philosophy without
> realising it.[1]

This means that all that has been achieved by philosophy will be
incorporated into future action, the revolution that is to put
Germany at the head of European progress. The only trouble with
Bauer's party, as Marx says in his next paragraph, is that they
'believed they could realise philosophy without abolishing it'.[2]

Bauer's influence was thus not something that Marx passed
through and then completely left behind: it was permanently
incorporated into his way of thinking. This influence can be seen
also in the Paris MSS. in spite of the scorn poured on 'critical
theologians'[3] in the preface. The central and all-inclusive position given here to the idea of communism proclaimed as the
solution to the riddle of history'[4] recalls the same place Bauer
gave to self-consciousness which he, too, described as 'the
solution of all riddles'.[5] The paradigmatic use that Marx made
of the criticism of religion is shown by the number of times

[1] Ibid. p. 495.   [2] Ibid. p. 496.   [3] Ibid. p. 508.
[4] Ibid. p. 594.   [5] B. Bauer, *Das entdeckte Christentum*, p. 160.

he introduces an economic point with a religious parallel. For example: 'just as in religion the spontaneous activity of human fantasy, of the human brain and heart, reacts independently as an alien activity, so the activity of the worker is not his spontaneous activity. It is another's activity and a loss of his own spontaneity'.[1] Similarly Marx comments on the fact that the worker is related to the product of his labour as to an alien object by saying that 'it is just the same as in religion. The more of himself man attributes to God the less he has left in himself'.[2] This makes plain the nature of Bauer's influence on Marx, an influence on the approach and structure of Marx's thought. A similar example would be the parallel between Bauer's 'catastrophic' view of the history of ideas and Marx's catastrophic view of the history of classes. The plot is the same though the characters are very different.

By the end of 1844 Marx and Engels felt obliged to render account publicly of their disagreements with Bruno Bauer and the Berlin Young Hegelians. This they did in *Die heilige Familie*, a work which, as regards similarity between Bauer's thought and that of Marx, contains little of interest since Marx is taking issue with a position of Bauer's very different from that which he held during their years of close contact. Thereafter Marx has hardly any reference to Bauer, though Engels always acknowledged a debt to his researches on the origins of the Gospels. There is no doubt that this is Bauer's major contribution and the one to which he was the most attached, a work that Schweitzer has called 'the ablest and most complete collection of the difficulties of the life of Jesus which is anywhere to be found'.[3]

As long as the Young Hegelians were of any importance in Germany Bruno Bauer was pre-eminent among them and appreciated even by men like Rosenkranz who had little in common with their way of thinking yet who could write that 'among the so-called "Free Thinkers" in Berlin Bruno Bauer is undoubtedly the most important, in character as in culture and talent'.[4] It would be a mistake to allow his difference in subject matter to obscure the influence of Bauer on some of the patterns of Marx's thinking.

[1] K. Marx, op. cit. p. 565.   [2] K. Marx, op. cit. p. 562.
[3] A. Schweitzer, *The Quest of the Historical Jesus* (London, 1954) p. 159.
[4] K. Rosenkranz, *Aus einem Tagebuch* (Leipzig, 1853) p. 113.

11. EDGAR BAUER AND MARX

Edgar Bauer, eleven years younger than Bruno, began by studying theology in Berlin, but then gave up and turned to history in
1839. This in turn he gave up and supported himself by giving
private lessons and proof-reading, while writing pamphlets in
support of his brother. One of these caused him to be arrested
and after a long trial he went to prison in 1846 for three years.
Later he split completely with Bruno and Egbert and returned to
orthodox Christianity. During his years in Berlin, however,
Edgar Bauer was one of the most prominent members of the
Graduates Club and composed with Engels a satirical poem on
Bruno Bauer's dismissal entitled *Der Triumph des Glaubens*. He
was the most politically minded writer of the Berlin Young
Hegelians.

In February 1842 he decided to devote himself to a criticism of
the South German liberals 'because of their want of doctrinal
vigour'. He called them the men of the *Juste Milieu* and in an
article of that title published in the *Rheinische Zeitung* in June
1842 he said: 'The *Juste Milieu* is the exact opposite of history
that pushes principles to their extremes . . . history loves oppositions, for it is by them that she develops'.[1] It is only extremes
that realise the importance of a revolution, for they alone have a
principle. This knowledge is vital, for it is the character of the age
to be revolutionary. Everything that lies between the two
extremes is mediocre and bad, mere hesitation and fear.

In his largest work on liberalism,[2] these two principles are
incorporated in people and government, which can never be reconciled. The ideal is for the people to absorb the government, but
constitutionalism makes the people only one of several parties in
the state. The only solution is for the people to become the chief
power, then the government will come from it by free election and
be merely an executive power at the service of the people. This
will be a government of the people or better: there will be no
government. But the so-called liberal 'realism', by blurring the
lines of opposition, impedes any genuine progress. This position

[1] E. Bauer, 'Das Juste-Milieu', in *Rheinische Zeitung*, 5 June 1842.
[2] Cf. E. Bauer, *Die liberalen Bestrebungen in Deutschland* (Zürich and
Winterthur, 1843).

reached its culmination in the book that Edgar Bauer wrote after the suppression of the radical press early in 1843, *Der Streit der Kritik mit Kirche und Staat*: 'only extremism can assume and carry through a principle in its purity; only extremism has the power to create. A principle never mediates; it only destroys, and its inner strength is proportionate to its destructive power'.[1]

The most striking thing about this book, which was viewed as communist propaganda by contemporaries, is the way in which it anticipates many of the positions of Marx in his *Einleitung zur Kritik der Hegelschen Rechtsphilosophie* and the Paris MSS. There is the same view of the preliminary and at the same time paradigmatic function of criticism of religion which is, according to Edgar Bauer, too, the 'presupposition of all criticism'.[2] The opening words of the *Einleitung* echo this. The importance of this article in Marx's development is that here for the first time, rejecting any purely political solution, he proclaims his adherence to the cause of the proletariat, his vision of the proletariat as the vehicle of salvation, the means of translating theory into practice.

It is quite likely that Edgar Bauer took a lot of his ideas from Weitling's book *Garantien der Harmonie und der Freiheit* which had appeared in December 1842 at the height of Weitling's agitations and influence. Weitling had laid great stress on the evil of private property, the division of society into warring classes whose actions were determined by economic factors, and the oppressive role of the state acting in the interests of the dominant class. Weitling hoped for a spontaneous revolt of the oppressed to put an end to all injustices and advocated it with a pathos very close to Edgar Bauer's.

Edgar Bauer, like Marx, believed in the imminence of a catastrophe, and not merely a theoretical one: 'In the inmost part of the state a chasm will open which . . . , with an earthquake that will shake to ruins our aristocratic framework, will send forth the hordes of the oppressed against law-protected egoism'.[3] In his opinion, as in Marx's, the time for the transition from theory to practice had arrived: 'Now criticism does not any longer merely send idea against idea, it sends into the field men against men . . . it finds in the practical force that it wields the proof of its own

[1] E. Bauer, *Der Streit der Kritik mit Kirche und Staat* (Bern, 1844) p. 93.
[2] Ibid. p. 331.   [3] Ibid. p. 315.

G

power'.[1] Edgar Bauer is clear, too, as to what sort of men will effect the revolution: the proletariat. 'It is the propertyless whose vocation it is to put an end to the pride of privilege'.[2] 'We find the practical beginning of the practical force for change in those who have suffered most under the old régime – the propertyless'.[3] The immediate aim is anarchy, 'the beginning of all good things'.[4] No private property, no privilege, no class distinction, no usurpatory government: that was Bauer's pronunciamento and he believed that history would bring about its realisation. It implied communism: 'Where everything is to be held in common, where the goods of the spirit are to be divided equally, property also must be held in common'.[5] Private property is the root of all evil: it makes society into a perpetual field of struggle that only the authority of the state can turn into an uneasy armistice. It makes men to be controlled by circumstances instead of the reverse. Nor is it only those without property who are thus affected: the men of property are equally enthralled. Ideas of reason and all thought, according to Bauer, are never something absolute, but always children of their times and circumstances. Past circumstances have produced private property and thereby all the evils of states, laws and crimes that depend on it. But not for ever – for property and propertylessness are inevitably pressing forward to a dissolution of these circumstances and the growing gap between rich and poor will very soon bring the propertyless to a realisation of their rights.

This impassioned and disjointed book cannot have been without a considerable influence on Marx seeing how many of his doctrines it anticipates, and it is ironical that he should so closely have appropriated ideas that a year before he had rejected in his public break with the 'Free Thinkers'.

[1] E. Bauer, Review of A. Alison, 'Geschichte Europas seit der ersten französischen Revolution', in *Deutsche Jahrbücher* (1842) p. 118.
[2] E. Bauer, *Der Streit der Kritik mit Kirche und Staat* (Bern, 1844) p. 315.
[3] Ibid. p. 323.
[4] Ibid. p. 294.
[5] Ibid. p. 289.

LUDWIG
FEUERBACH

1. FEUERBACH'S EARLY WRITINGS

LUDWIG FEUERBACH was born in 1804 into a family many of whose members were to distinguish themselves in very different ways. His father was an eminent jurist whose biography and writings Feuerbach published after his death in 1852. His brother Karl was a mathematician who committed suicide when arrested for liberal activities, his elder brother Anselm was a theologian who turned to mysticism and his nephew Anselm was one of the best-known painters in Germany during the last century.

Feuerbach's whole work was dominated by one idea – that of religion. He wrote in 1848: 'All my writings have only one aim, one design, one object. This is precisely religion, theology and anything connected with them'.[1] Add to this a passage from a very early letter to his father and the essential lines of Feuerbach's thought are already drawn: 'I wish to press to my heart nature, from whose depths the frightened theologian shies away, and man, the whole man, not man as dealt with by the theologian, anatomist or lawyer, but as object of philosophy'.[2] In accordance with these ideas, Feuerbach began his career by studying Protestant theology at the University of Heidelberg. There he found the lectures of Paulus, the rationalist theologian, extremely empty and appreciated only Daub, whose speculative treatment of religion interested him in philosophy. He then went to Berlin and, while trying to keep up his theology, attended Hegel's lectures which were a great illumination to him: 'What in Daub seemed to me to be still dark and unintelligible, or at least un-

[1] L. Feuerbach, *Sämtliche Werke*, VIII, p. 6.   [2] Ibid. II, p. 362.

founded, I have now understood clearly and realised its necessity
simply as a result of the few lectures I have heard from Hegel'.[1]
Hegel was, according to Feuerbach, much clearer in his lectures
than in his writings, and Feuerbach studied under him for two
years during which time he gave up the study of theology completely.

Feuerbach thought of himself as Hegel's direct disciple and his
dissertation, presented in 1828 at the University of Erlangen, is
conceived in a fully Hegelian manner: its title is *De ratione, una,
universa et infinita*, and exalts the all-powerfulness and self-
sufficiency of reason, the only point of difference with Hegel being
that Feuerbach did not consider (as did Hegel) that Christianity
could be the perfect religion for 'this could only be the domain
of the real idea and existing reason'.[2] On gaining his doctorate
Feuerbach began lecturing at the university in the hope of later
obtaining a chair there.

The next decade was a very mixed one, both in Feuerbach's
own thinking and in his career. In 1830 he published anonymously a book called *Gedanken über Tod und Unsterblichkeit* in
which he dealt with one of the questions obviously raised by
Hegel's philosophy of religion: the immortality of the soul.
Feuerbach here argues against any sort of individual immortality,
only immortality of the human spirit as a whole being possible,
and replaces divine transcendance by human transcendance.
His veil of anonymity was pierced and, as his father predicted,
the book cost him his university career and for the next few years
he led a roving life, living in Frankfurt, Erlangen, Ansbach and
Nürnberg in succession.

However, when he was invited in 1834 by de Henning, editor
of the influential orthodox Hegelian *Jahrbücher*, to reply to an
attack on the Master by Bachmann, who wished to substitute
for Hegel's speculation a sort of dogmatic realism, Feuerbach
responded with a complete vindication of Hegel. Only spirit, he
said, was capable of explaining and justifying matter. Hunger,
thirst, perception are secondary: the true being of man is universal
reason. Following the writing of this article and on the advice
of his relatives, Feuerbach again took up lecturing at Erlangen,
and published volumes on Leibniz and Bayle that gained the

---

[1] Ibid. ii, p. 361.　　　　[2] Ibid. iv, p. 361.

praise of the Prussian minister for Culture, Altenstein. In these books Feuerbach elaborated on the theme common to all the Young Hegelians, the incompatibility of philosophy and religion.

It was at this time that Arnold Ruge was looking for subscribers to his new *Hallische Jahrbücher* and asked Feuerbach if he would contribute. He agreed and was henceforth closely associated with the Young Hegelian movement. Nevertheless, his first contribution to the *Jahrbücher* remained very close to Hegel, defending him against the attack of a certain Dorguth whose book advocated a sort of physiological empiricism. During the argument between Leo and the Young Hegelians Feuerbach contributed an essay on philosophy and Christianity in which he emphasised ever more strongly their incompatibility, thus foreshadowing his later reinstatement of religion as a purely human affair of the heart. In this article Feuerbach was still prepared to defend Hegel against Leo's attacks. But in 1839 Feuerbach dealt directly with Hegel's philosophy for the first time in a long article entitled 'Zur Kritik der Hegelschen Philosophie' which starts many of the themes that are at the basis of Feuerbach's thinking for the next few years – the description of Hegel's philosophy as 'rational mysticism', the criticism that Hegel eclipses material reality, and the advocacy of a return to nature in all its fullness.

It was solely by means of his writings that Feuerbach influenced his fellow Young Hegelians. His marriage in 1837 with the daughter of an inspector of a porcelain factory permitted him to retire to a farm in the same village as the factory where he remained until the late 1850s, completely cut off from the activities of the rest of the world. Feuerbach was never tired of praising his retreat at Bruckberg and the isolation and nearness to nature undoubtedly had a great effect on his philosophy.

2. 'DAS WESEN DES CHRISTENTUMS'

In April 1841 Feuerbach published what was to be his most influential work – *Das Wesen des Christentums*. This book continues the critical study of Christianity already made by Strauss and Bruno Bauer, but at the same time has a more general approach, as Feuerbach claimed in his preface to the second edition:

> As far as concerns my position with regard to Strauss and Bruno Bauer . . . Bauer concentrates his criticism on the history of the Gospels, that is biblical Christianity, or rather biblical theology, while Strauss deals with Christian dogma, that is dogmatic Christianity or rather dogmatic theology. I, on the other hand, deal with Christianity in a general manner, that is the Christian religion, and the philosophy and theology only as a consequence of this. . . . My principal interest is Christianity and religion in so far as it is the immediate object, the immediate essence of man.[1]

The main point of *Das Wesen des Christentums* is that religion does indeed reveal the essence of man, but that if this essence is viewed as more truly belonging to God, then man is deprived of it. Man is separated from himself and becomes alienated. The richer is God, the poorer is man. Feuerbach himself, in a letter to Wigand, his publisher, described the 'fundamental idea' of the book as follows:

> The objective essence of religion, particularly the Christian religion, is nothing but the essence of human, and particularly Christian feeling, the secret of theology therefore is anthropology. . . . The foundation of a new science is laid here in that the philosophy of religion is conceived of and presented as esoteric or secret anthropology or psychology.[2]

This is direct opposition to Hegel's philosophy of religion. In the introduction to his lectures on this subject Hegel had objected against religion's being taken from the sphere of reason to be put in that of the 'arbitrary subjectivity of feeling'. Those whose idea of God was exclusively produced by feeling would end up with a God who was a product of weakness, hope and joy, and this led to atheism. Hegel had in mind here the disciples of Schleiermacher, but it was Feuerbach who brought this prophecy to ful-

[1] L. Feuerbach, *Das Wesen des Christentums*, 2nd ed. (Leipzig, 1843) pp. xixf.

[2] L. Feuerbach, *Briefwechsel*, ed. Schuffenhauer (Leipzig, 1963) pp. 140f.

filment. For Feuerbach, what was religious had an exclusively
emotional character and thus a character completely separate
from rational thought. His view can be summed up in the
sentence: 'The basic dogmas of Christianity are the fulfilled
wishes of mankind. The essence of Christianity is the essence of
feeling'.[1]

The book is divided into two parts, the first a constructive one,
the reduction of religion to what Feuerbach considered to be its
essence, the second more destructive, an analysis of the contradictions involved in theology. The first half is the more important:
Feuerbach is concerned here to show that the qualities of the
divinity – foresight, planned direction of the future, goodness,
justice, love and holiness – are in fact objectified qualities of the
human race. As a conclusion to the first half of his book Feuerbach writes: 'We have reduced the other-worldly, supernatural
and superhuman essence of God to its particular foundations in
the essence of man. Thus we have in the end arrived back at our
starting point. Man is the beginning of religion, Man is the
centre of religion, Man is the end of religion'.[2] God is merely an
imaginary representation of the perfections that are lacking
among mankind, thus nothing objective, only an idea, though
man is not, of course, conscious of this. This idea of God becomes
independent of the minds that create it and the original relation
of subject and object is reversed. Sometimes, though rarely,
Feuerbach speaks as though these imaginings had themselves bad
effects, as though God and man were in competition. He says,
for example: 'so that God may be enriched, man will have to be
impoverished'. And in the conclusion to the book he says that
the divine essence is indeed in reality human, but 'religion is not
aware of the humanity of its content; it is rather opposed to what
is human, or at least does not admit that its content is a human
one'.[3] Feuerbach proclaimed that the time was now ripe to
reclaim the alienated attributes of man and so recover the unity
with God that had characterised the beginnings of human
history: 'The necessary turning point of history is this plain
confession and admission that the essence of God is nothing but

[1] L. Feuerbach, *Das Wesen des Christentums*, 2nd ed. (Leipzig, 1843)
pp. xixf.

[2] L. Feuerbach, *Sämtliche Werke*, vi, p. 222.   [3] Ibid. vi, p. 325.

the consciousness of the human species'.[1] The question of the origin of these imaginings is not dealt with at all in *Das Wesen des Christentums*, but only in later writings where Feuerbach says that men recognise in God what they find missing in themselves: 'It is only human misery that affords God his birthplace'.[2]

An extremely important point to bear in mind (particularly concerning the influence of the book that Engels tried to represent as 'materialist') is that Feuerbach made considerable changes in *Das Wesen des Christentums* in successive editions. The first edition was still considerably under the influence of Hegel, indeed even marked a slight return to Hegel as compared with the 'Kritik der Hegelschen Philosophie' of two years earlier. In his introduction to the first edition Feuerbach surprisingly concurs in Hegel's fundamental view of religion: 'Of course it is self-evident that philosophy and religion in general, that is apart from their specific differences, are identical, and that, since it is one and the same being which both thinks and believes so do the pictures of religion express thoughts and things'.[3] And later in the same introduction he refers to Hegel's method in treating of man's attitude to theology as 'perfectly correct and historically grounded'.[4] In several passages, too, Feuerbach refers to 'reason' as the moving force of the universe, as for example: 'Thus reason is the all-pitying being, the love of the universe for itself. To reason alone is given the task of raising up all beings, of redeeming and reconciling them'.[5] Certainly later Feuerbach was very dissatisfied with the 'idealistic' elements in *Das Wesen des Christentums* and preferred his later, more materialist, treatises on the nature of religion. In his letter to Wigand Feuerbach described the book as 'speculatively empirical' and 'speculatively rational' and intended, if the book were not published anonymously,[6] that it should have as its title: 'Philosophy of Religion from the Standpoint of Speculative Rationalism'.[7]

Feuerbach's work is often regarded as atheistic, but he indignantly repudiated this term. The first half of *Das Wesen des*

---

[1] L. Feuerbach, *Sämtliche Werke*, vi, p. 325.   [2] Ibid. ii, p. 292.
[3] L. Feuerbach, *Das Wesen des Christentums* (Leipzig, 1841) p. iv.
[4] Ibid. p. viii.   [5] Ibid. p. 384.
[6] L. Feuerbach, *Briefwechsel* (Leipzig, 1963) p. 142.
[7] Ibid. p. 144.

Christentums bears the title 'The True, that is Anthropological
Nature of Religion' and Feuerbach's declared aim was to achieve
the unity of God and man that he believed existed at the beginning of history. The closing sentences of the book – sentences
which Ruge begged Feuerbach to suppress – had a very religious
tone: 'We have only to interrupt the normal and common course
of things to find in what is ordinary a particular importance, and
in life as such an overall religious importance. Let therefore not
only bread and wine be sacred to us, but water as well'.[1] Feuerbach did not envisage a time when there would be no more religion
– he did not advocate its abolition, merely its purification.
Feuerbach's use of words is never very precise, and sometimes it
sounds as though he is against any and all manifestations of
religion. But other passages force one to conclude that all that he
was opposed to was what he conceived to be the detrimental side
of religion – what he more usually referred to as 'theology'. He
himself viewed his contribution as a very positive one: 'My
explanation of religion is a reproduction of the religious principle
at its source and, starting from the origin of the ideas of modern
man on nature and himself, a purification of religion from its
manifestations that are in absolute contradiction with it, but
certainly not total negation'. And again: 'Our attitude to
religion is therefore not a negative one, but a critical one; we only
divide the true from the false'.[2] This fundamental ambivalence
with regard to religion was what so annoyed Max Stirner and led
him to describe Feuerbach as a 'pious atheist'. Indeed, sometimes
Feuerbach speaks of his own philosophy as a new religion. 'The
new philosophy takes the place of religion, it contains in itself the
essence of religion, it is in truth itself religion'.[3] This attitude of
Feuerbach's was also to have very important consequences for his
socialist followers, the so-called 'true socialists', Hess and Grün.
Their acceptance of Feuerbach's attitude to religion and morality,
their belief in eternal values, was one of the major causes of their
break with Marx.

It is also worth while enlarging on what Feuerbach says about
the term 'species' (*Gattung*). The word had been popularised by
D. F. Strauss who, in the well-known conclusion to his *Das Leben*

[1] L. Feuerbach, *Sämtliche Werke*, vi, p. 335.
[2] Ibid. vi, p. 326.   [3] Ibid. ii, p. 319f.

Jesu, said: 'It is not the way in which the idea realises itself to pour out its whole fullness in one example ... rather it likes to spread out its riches in the multiplicity of examples which mutually complete themselves'. And he continues: 'When thought of as belonging to an individual, a God-man, the qualities and function that the teaching of the Church attributes to Christ are contradictory, but in the species they live in harmony. Humanity is the unity of both natures, finite spirit remembering its infinity'.[1]

This is taken up by Feuerbach in his writings before *Das Wesen des Christentums* and then in that work is introduced at the very beginning to suggest how man is to be distinguished from other animals: man is conscious of himself not only as an individual, but also as a member of the human species. Feuerbach then applies the idea to religion by saying that God is really the perfected idea of the species viewed as an individual: God embraces all perfections as the species is capable of doing. The fundamental unity of mankind that the idea of a species presupposes arises from the fact that men are not self-sufficient creatures; they have very different qualities, so it is only together that they can form the 'perfect' man. For Feuerbach all knowledge comes to man as a member of the human species and when man acts as a member of the human species his action is qualitatively different. His fellow human beings make him conscious of himself as a man, they form his consciousness and even the criterion of truth. 'The species', says Feuerbach, 'is the last measure of truth ... what is true is what is in agreement with the essence of the species, what is false is what disagrees with it'. The idea of God only arises because the human species has not yet realised its own perfection. After *Das Wesen des Christentums* Feuerbach no longer used the word 'species' but replaced it with 'community' and also tended to speak about the relations of two people viewed apart from the rest of society.

3. INFLUENCE OF 'DAS WESEN DES CHRISTENTUMS'

Das Wesen des Christentums was published in November 1841, a little after Marx submitted his doctoral dissertation. Marx had

[1] D. F. Strauss, *Das Leben Jesu* (Tübingen, 1836) II, pp. 734 ff.

certainly read Feuerbach before submitting his dissertation; he refers to his *Geschichte der neueren Philosophie*. Most commentators have attributed a permanent importance to the book and its influence on Marx. The chief reason for attributing such weight to *Das Wesen des Christentums* rather than Feuerbach's later writings is an emphatic passage in Engels' 'Ludwig Feuerbach und der Ausgang der klassischen deutschen Philosophie', a series of articles written as a review of a biography of Feuerbach. On the appearance of *Das Wesen des Christentums*, wrote Engels:

> The spell was broken: the 'system' was shattered and thrown aside, the contradiction resolved; for it existed only in the imagination. No one can have an idea of the liberating influence of this book unless he himself experienced it. Enthusiasm was general: we were all for the moment 'Feuerbachians'. A reading of *Die heilige Familie* will show with what enthusiasm Marx greeted the new approach, and how much – in spite of all his critical reserves – he was influenced by it.[1]

Engels' description of the effect of the book is completely at variance with the facts. So far from the 'system' being broken, the general opinion among the Young Hegelians was that Feuerbach's book was a continuation of Hegel's doctrines, much on the same lines as Bruno Bauer claimed for his *Posaune*. Ruge, standing, as editor of the *Hallische Jahrbücher*, at the crossroads of Young Hegelian opinion, speaks of Feuerbach's 'progress vis-à-vis Hegel',[2] of Strauss, Feuerbach and Bruno Bauer as 'the true interpreters of Hegel's philosophy'[3] and couples Feuerbach with Bruno Bauer in another letter. Indeed, a correspondent of the *Augsburger Allgemeine Zeitung* had gone so far, declared Feuerbach, 'as to dare to assert publicly that one need only read "a few pages" of my book to be convinced that the author is the same as the author of the *Posaune*'.[4]

Engels himself, in an article that was widely read and discussed, lavished praise on Feuerbach, but as a true disciple of Hegel, one

---

[1] F. Engels, *Ludwig Feuerbach und der Ausgang der klassischen deutschen Philosophie* (Berlin, 1886) p. 12f.

[2] A. Ruge, *Briefwechsel*, ɪ, p. 224.   [3] Ibid. p. 246.

[4] L. Feuerbach, *Briefwechsel u. Nachlass*, ed. Grün (Leipzig and Heidelberg, 1874) ɪ, p. 337.

who had given humanity 'a consciousness of itself'. The 'religion of every true philosopher' was still 'faith in the omnipotence of the idea and in the victory of eternal truth'.

This misinterpretation so annoyed Feuerbach that in the following year he published an article entitled 'Zur Beurteilung des Wesens des Christentums' in which he said:

> My philosophy of religion is so little a development of Hegel's ... that it sooner has its origin in an opposition to Hegel and can only be understood in the light of this opposition. [He then went on to point out in detail the nature of this opposition.] Hegel identifies religion with philosophy, I bring out their specific difference; Hegel criticises religion only in thought, I in its true essence; Hegel objectifies what is subjective, I subjectify what is objective. Hegel opposes the finite to the infinite, the speculative to the empirical, whereas I, precisely because I already find the infinite in the finite and the speculative in the empirical and because the infinite is for me merely the essence of the finite, find also in the speculative mysteries of religion nothing but empirical truths, as, for example, the only truth contained in the 'speculative mystery' of the Trinity is that communal life is the only form of life thus not a truth apart, transcendant and supernatural, but a general truth immanent to man, or, in popular terms, a natural truth.[1]

This passage, however, represents as much a change in Feuerbach's own opinions as an elucidation of previously held views. For the second edition of *Das Wesen des Christentums*, published in 1843, differed from the first in that several more prominent echoes of Hegel were omitted and the characterisation of the book in his letter to Wigand as 'speculatively empirical' and 'speculatively rational' expresses a position that Feuerbach had given up by 1843.

It is obvious from all this that Engels' description, written fifty years after the period it describes, bears little relation to the reality. This discrepancy is emphasised by his reference to *Die heilige Familie*, where Marx mentions not *Das Wesen des*

[1] L. Feuerbach, *Kleine philosophische Schriften*, ed. Lange (Leipzig, 1950) pp. 34ff.

Christentums as Engels implies, but Feuerbach's later writings which were much more important from Marx's point of view. The truth is that though *Das Wesen des Christentums* did have a wide public, it was one that accepted it as one radical commentary on Hegel among others. It was not until the beginning of 1843, when the radical movement began to realise its political failure and thus to lose its attachment to Hegel, that Feuerbach, more through writings subsequent to *Das Wesen des Christentums*, became the predominant influence among the Young Hegelians. It is significant that Moses Hess, as will be shown more fully later, did not become an exclusive disciple of Feuerbach until the very end of 1843. Of all the Young Hegelians *Das Wesen des Christentums* influenced Ruge the most, though he did not follow its doctrines very closely. From Feuerbach's conception of men's religious ideas being society's ideals, as yet unrealised on earth and thus reflected into another world, Ruge extracted a religion of politics whose object was the human spirit pressing forward with the progress of history.

The book, and Feuerbach's writings in general, had a more lasting effect on Engels than on Marx and he is generalising about an effect that was probably stronger on him than on most Young Hegelians. Marx in particular had made close studies of Hegel whose influence never left him, proving itself much deeper than that of Feuerbach. Engels, on the other hand, was an autodidact who had not been through the same academic discipline as Marx and thus was more open to Feuerbach's simple and popular style.

Also religion was a heart-rending problem for Engels in a way that it never was to Marx, as Engels' pathetic letters to the Gräber brothers show. He was much influenced by Strauss and Schleiermacher, but it was Feuerbach who finally provided him with a safe and secure solution to the religious problem. Engels' critique of Schelling, written in 1842, contains many echoes of Feuerbach and the poem *Triumph des Glaubens*, that he composed with Edgar Bauer, shows his admiration for the rugged independence of Feuerbach's humanism, and in his essays in the *Deutsch-französische Jahrbücher* he continues to celebrate Feuerbach's 'overcoming of pantheism'.[1]

To return to Marx: it was not that *Das Wesen des Christentums*

[1] Cf. Marx–Engels, *Werke* (Berlin, 1961) pp. 543 f.

had no influence on him, for its influence on him as on other Young
Hegelians was quite considerable and bore out Feuerbach's claim
prior to its publication that his book 'neither could nor ought to
be ignored'.[1] But neither was it as decisive as Engels would have
his readers believe, nor was its influence in the direction he states.
For the chief subject of the book, its critique of religion, was not
of paramount interest to Marx, as he had already learned atheism
from Bruno Bauer. What struck Marx much more was the
'humanism' of the book. Engels' emphasis is all wrong when he
says that *Das Wesen des Christentums* 'replaced an unqualified
materialism on the throne'.[2] The book was not materialist in the
normal sense of the word, for Feuerbach did not regard himself as
an atheist and, indeed, the closing words of the book had such a
religious sound that Ruge begged him to cut them out, though
Feuerbach, who did not have Ruge's political concern for the
immediate effect of writings, would not be persuaded to alter
anything. This ambivalence is characteristic of all Feuerbach's
writings during the period 1838–43. In the thirties Feuerbach
was an idealist and a Hegelian and in the late forties he became,
and remained, a materialist, but in the intervening years he
attempted to hold the very difficult balance between the two. He
himself, of course, preferred his later works on religion as they
were more materialist: *Das Wesen des Christentums* he regarded
as being spoilt by an idealistic residue. The book's original title
and its Hegelianism also preclude its being called materialist.
Feuerbach did not intend to exalt any one aspect of man at the
expense of others: he wanted man to reclaim for himself the whole
of his being, including its religious aspect. Such specific borrowings by Marx, as can be traced to *Das Wesen des Christentums*,
all have this slant: the very first pages contain the idea of man's
being distinguished from an animal by his consciousness of himself as the member of a species. This was taken straight over by
Marx in 'Die Judenfrage' and developed in the Paris MSS. A
similar desire to relate everything to human perception and action
inspires Marx's assertion in the Paris MSS, that man has his
nature outside himself, that is in contact with other beings, for

[1] L. Feuerbach, *Briefwechsel* (Leipzig, 1963) p. 143.
[2] F. Engels, *Ludwig Feuerbach und der Ausgang der klassischen deutschen
Philosophie* (Berlin, 1886) p. 12.

'a non-objective being is a non-being'[1] – the very same words as Feuerbach used to attack the idea of a God who entertained no relations with men. This same attitude to Feuerbach comes out clearly in a little article written at the beginning of 1842 and published a year later, where, on the question of miracles, Marx praises the view of Feuerbach who 'cuts the argument short and says: a miracle is the realisation of a natural or human wish in a supernatural manner'.[2]

In the same article Marx declares his enthusiasm for Feuerbach's ideas by saying that their acceptance is absolutely necessary for those who wish to accede to the truth:

> To you, speculative theologians and philosophers, I give this advice: free yourselves from the concepts and prejudices of previous speculative philosophy if you wish really to discover things as they are, that is if you wish to discover the truth. And there is no other way to truth and freedom than through the 'river of fire'.[3] Feuerbach is the purgatory of the present time.[4]

It should be remembered that at the time of writing this Marx was still collaborating with Bruno Bauer on the second part of the *Posaune* and would certainly not have regarded himself as any kind of a materialist. This term cannot be applied to any of his writings until *Die heilige Familie*, and Marx himself twice rejects it in the Paris MSS.

4. 'VORLAÜFIGE THESEN' AND 'GRUNDSÄTZE'

The articles that Marx wrote for the *Rheinische Zeitung* in 1842 show no trace of Feuerbach's influence and it is only in 1843 that Marx produces something whose inspiration is plainly Feuerbachian – his unfinished commentary on Hegel's *Rechtsphilosophie*. This Marx wrote at Kreuznach from March to August 1843 and it was during this time too that Feuerbach published two writings

[1] K. Marx, *Frühe Schriften*, I, p. 651.   [2] Ibid. p. 107.
[3] The literal meaning of 'Feuerbach'.
[4] K. Marx, *Frühe Schriften*, I, p. 109.

that were, from Marx's point of view, his most important:
'Vorlaüfige Thesen zur Reform der Philosophie' and 'Grundsätze
der Philosophie der Zukunft'.

The 'Thesen' were written in April 1842 and published in
Ruge's collection *Anekdota* in February 1843. At the very
beginning Feuerbach makes clear the connexion between this
article and *Das Wesen des Christentums*. He says: 'the secret of
theology is anthropology, but the secret of speculative philosophy
is theology'.[1] Feuerbach is now going to deal with speculative
philosophy in the same way as he has dealt with theology. The
speculative philosophy *par excellence* is the Hegelian and the
method of criticism in the two fields is the same: the same
reversal of subject and object will uncover the truth. Since
Hegel's logic is merely theology turned into a reasonable and
relevant form, man can only reclaim his essence by a total transformation of the Hegelian philosophy, a transformation that will
bring to light the truth that is nevertheless contained in it.

> The identification with man of his essence that abstraction has
> taken away from him can only be fully understood and con-
> ceived when it is understood as a total negation of speculative
> philosophy, although it is at the same time the truth of this
> philosophy. Indeed, everything is contained in Hegel's
> philosophy but is accompanied at the same time by its nega-
> tion, its opposite.[2]
>
> The beginning of philosophy is the limited, the finite, the
> real.[3]

Hegel's logic contained the essence of man and nature, 'but without man and without nature'.[4] What Hegel relegated to a footnote must now be included in the text of philosophy. Philosophy
has to begin with what is not philosophy – the primacy of the
senses. This had mainly developed in France and was a good
antidote to German metaphysics. Thus the true philosopher
would have to be of 'Franco-Germanic blood'. Hegel's philosophy
had indeed abolished the contradiction between thought and
being, but always within the limits of thought. Anyone who does
not give up Hegel's philosophy cannot give up theology either,

[1] L. Feuerbach, *Sämtliche Werke*, ii, p. 222.   [2] Ibid. p. 227.
[3] Ibid. p. 230.   [4] Ibid. p. 234.

for Hegel's philosophy is the last refuge, the last rational support of theology. Feuerbach formulates his general point of view thus: 'Thus true relationship of thought to being is this: being is the subject, thought the predicate. Thought arises from being, being does not arise from thought'.[1] The essence of being is nature, which is also the ground of man. Thus the only principle of the new philosophy is 'thinking man himself'.[2] In what is obviously a reference to Bruno Bauer, Feuerbach says: 'If we translate "man" by "self-consciousness", then this is to relegate the new philosophy to the point of view of the old; for the self-consciousness of the old philosophy separated from man is an abstraction without reality. Man is self-consciousness'.[3]

The 'Grundsätze', published in July 1843, are a continuation and more detailed working-out of the 'Thesen', and their purpose was 'to deduce from the philosophy of the absolute, that is theology, the necessity of the philosophy of man, that is anthropology, and through a critique of the divine philosophy to lay the foundation for a critique of a human one'.[4]

This deeper version of the 'Thesen' consists mainly of a criticism of past philosophies and there are many repetitions. As in the 'Thesen' Feuerbach begins by demonstrating that the essence of speculative philosophy is just the same as that of theology, except that it has been rationalised. While in theism God is a being existing outside reason, in speculative philosophy reason has become God and thus the subject.

Feuerbach then proceeds to deal explicitly with Hegel's philosophy whose great fault, according to him, is its negation of theology 'from the standpoint of theology'.[5] Hegel has merely got rid of the subject in Fichte's subjective idealism and is very near to the Neoplatonists – Feuerbach calls him the German Proclus. Hegel may have been a realist, but he was always an abstract realist who never managed to break out of the circle of pure ideas: 'If the reality of thought is merely thought reality, then the reality of thought is still merely a thought and we are still imprisoned within the identity of thought with itself, inside idealism'.[6]

[1] Ibid. p. 239. [2] Ibid. p. 241.
[3] Ibid. p. 242. [4] Ibid. p. 245.
[5] Ibid. p. 275. [6] Ibid. p. 294.

H

Feuerbach now expounds his own views and sets out his 'new' philosophy: 'The new philosophy deals with being as it is for us, not only as thinking, but as really existing being – being, that is, as object of being, being as object of itself. Being as object of being, – and only this being, is the primary being and deserves the name – it is the being of the senses, sight, feeling and love'.[1] Feuerbach attaches great importance to this latter, even speaking of it as a criterion of existence. 'The old philosophers said: what is not thought, does not exist; the new philosopher says on the contrary: what is not loved, what cannot be loved, that does not exist'.[2] The ultimate criterion of judgement is not the self, not reason, but man with all his manifold qualities. The old philosophers said that only the rational was true and real, whereas the new philosopher says that only the human is true and real; since only what is human is rational, and man is the measure of reason. 'The unity of thought and being only has meaning and truth when man is conceived of as the foundation and subject of this unity'.[3] 'Man' here certainly does not mean the individual, for man's essence is a communal one – 'the essence of man is contained in community, in the unity of man with man'. On this note the 'Grundsätze' end. That Feuerbach considered it to be a complete break with the past is shown by the concluding words: 'the necessary condition for a really new and independent philosophy to meet the needs of humanity and the future is that it be essentially different from the old philosophy'.[4]

It is interesting to note that even here Feuerbach's concept of 'materialism' is an extremely imprecise one, for he uses the word in very different senses. At the beginning of *Das Wesen des Christentums* materialism is coupled with scepticism and pantheism and a little later on it is even equated with love. At the end of the same book he affirms that man belongs to the essence of nature as a point against what he refers to as 'vulgar materialism'. In the 'Grundsätze' the essence of modern times is described as 'the divinisation of the real, materialism, empiricism, realism, humanism',[5] and on the next page there is the following disarming footnote: 'The differences between materialism, empiri-

---

[1] Ibid. p. 297.   [2] Ibid. p. 299.
[3] L. Feuerbach *Sämtliche Werke*, II, p. 313.
[4] Ibid. p. 320.   [5] Ibid. p. 265.

cism, realism and humanism are of course in this article of no importance'.[1]

5. Influence of the 'Thesen' and 'Grundsätze' on Marx

It can be shown both that Feuerbach had a very strong influence on Marx during the years 1843–5 and that this influence was principally that of the 'Thesen' and the 'Grundsätze'. The best way to see this clearly is firstly to examine closely Marx's chief reference to Feuerbach's work and secondly to trace the influence of Feuerbach's work in what Marx wrote during these years.

Marx's most explicit reference to Feuerbach comes at the end of the Paris MSS., where he mentions the two writings here in question: 'Feuerbach, in his "Thesen" in the *Anekdota* and, in greater detail, in his "Philosophie der Zukunft" has demolished the inner principle of the old dialectic and philosophy'.[2] And later:

Feuerbach is the only person who has a serious and critical relation to Hegel's dialectic, who has made real discoveries in this field, and above all, who has vanquished the old philosophy. The magnitude of Feuerbach's achievement and the unassuming simplicity with which he presents his work are in striking contrast with the behaviour of others.

Feuerbach's great achievement is:

1. to have shown that philosophy is nothing more than religion brought into thought and developed by thought, and that it is equally to be condemned as another form and mode of existence of human alienation;

2. to have founded genuine materialism and positive science by making the social relationship of 'man to man' the basic principle of his theory;

3. to have opposed to the negation of the negation which claims to be the absolute positive, a self-subsistent principle founded on itself.[3]

[1] Ibid. p. 266. [2] K. Marx, *Frühe Schriften*, I, p. 638.
[3] Ibid. p. 639.

It is revealing that each one of these points in Feuerbach's 'great achievement' comes either from the 'Thesen' or from the 'Grundsätze':

1. That Hegelian philosophy is to be condemned as an alienation just as much as religion is the whole theme of the 'Thesen', with their assertion that the same criticisms apply to both of them and their description of Hegel's philosophy as the last rational support of religion.

2. Feuerbach 'makes the social relationship of "man to man" the basic principle of his theory towards the end of the "Grundsätze" where he says, for instance, "ideas have their sole origin in the sharing and conversation of man with man. Man cannot create rational concepts in isolation. . . . The community of man with man is the first principle and sole criterion of truth"'.[1]

3. The third point is a little obscure as it stands, but is expounded by Marx somewhat further on where he says that the positing or affirmation contained in the negation of the negation is still uncertain and incomplete. It is not demonstrated by its own existence and explicit. It is the direct opposite of the positing which is perceptually indubitable and grounded upon itself, and the example he gives is the reintegration of religion and theology into the final system of Hegel after their initial negation. This, too, is taken from the 'Grundsätze' where Feuerbach says that, according to Hegel:

God is God in that he supersedes matter, the negation of God. And only the negation of the negation is the true affirmation. So finally we are where we were at the beginning – in the bosom of Christian theology. In the last analysis, the secret of the Hegelian dialectic is just this, that it negates theology by philosophy and then again negates philosophy by theology.[2]

This view of the strong influence of the 'Thesen' and 'Grundsätze' is also borne out by a close study of Marx's writings in the years 1843–5.

The first of Marx's writings to show a strong influence of Feuerbach was his *Kritik des Hegelschen Staatsrechts* written during the middle months of 1843, an unfinished MS. comprising

[1] L. Feuerbach, *Sämtliche Werke*, ii, p. 304.   [2] Ibid. pp. 276 f.

a paragraph by paragraph commentary on Hegel's text. In his commentary on that paragraph of Hegel which he says contains the whole mystery of Hegel's *Rechtsphilosophie*, Marx writes:

> The idea is made into a subject and the true relationship of family and civil society to the state is conceived of as the inner, imaginary activity of the idea. Family and civil society are presuppositions of the state; they are the real agents; but speculation reverses their roles. . . . The facts that are the basis of everything are not thought of as such, but as a mystical result.[1]

It is inaccurate to say of this writing of Marx's that it transfers Feuerbach's criticism of religion to the sphere of politics. But, though of course Marx is here influenced by the thought of Feuerbach in general, the work that most immediately influenced him was the 'Thesen', which had been published just before Marx began to write. The 'Thesen' are a general criticism of Hegelian philosophy: Marx applies this same criticism to Hegel's political philosophy. Some of Marx's most characteristic terminology is taken over straight from the 'Thesen'. For example, in the quotation above, and frequently elsewhere, Marx accused Hegel of having reversed the proper relation of subject and object, by making the idea or the state the cause instead of the effect: 'The important thing is that Hegel everywhere makes the idea into the subject and thus the real, proper subject into the predicate'.[2] This makes specific Feuerbach's criticism at the beginning of the 'Thesen': 'We need only make the predicate into the subject and thus reverse speculative philosophy in order to arrive at the unconcealed, pure and naked truth'.[3] Another favourite accusation of Marx is that of mystification: 'Hegel's aim is to give the political constitution a relationship to the abstract idea, to fit it in as part of the life history of the idea – an obvious mystification'.[4] This concept, too, was taken from Feuerbach according to whom 'mystification' was the result of the wrong relationship of subject to predicate. The true subject – man and his relation to other men and to nature – was mystified

---

[1] K. Marx, *Frühe Schriften*, i, pp. 262 ff.   [2] Ibid. p. 266.
[3] L. Feuerbach, *Sämtliche Werke*, ii, p. 224.
[4] K. Marx, op. cit. p. 272.

by being turned into the mere predicate of the idea. Marx, in his demand for basing the state on the 'reality' of man, is following Feuerbach's accusation against Hegel that he had alienated man from himself by putting man's essence outside man himself. For Feuerbach, as for Marx, 'man is the foundation of the state'.[1]

Marx's general contrast of the concrete reality against the 'abstractions' of Hegel is inspired by Feuerbach's assertion in the 'Thesen' that 'the beginning of philosophy is not God, not the absolute, not being as the predicate of the absolute or the idea, the beginning of philosophy is the finite, the definite, the real'.[2]

In Marx's essay 'Zur Judenfrage' the same idea of the state as the alienation of man's essence is put forward in a less abstruse and more pointed fashion. Feuerbach's influence is particularly apparent here through the work of Moses Hess of whose application to the field of economics of Feuerbach's doctrine of alienation Marx makes the fullest use. Marx also takes up the idea from *Das Wesen des Christentums* of man as a being who accomplishes himself in and through his species – man as a 'species-being'. Marx writes at the end of the first part of his 'Judenfrage':

> Human emancipation will only be complete when the real, individual man has absorbed into himself the abstract citizen; when, as an individual man, in his everyday life, in his work, in his relationships, he has become a species-being; and when he has recognised and organized his own powers as social powers so that he no longer separates this social power from himself as political power.[3]

Feuerbach had laid great emphasis on this idea in the opening pages of *Das Wesen des Christentums* in an argument to show that it is consciousness of himself as a species-being that differentiates man from other animals. It was in employing this expression that Marx most clearly proclaimed himself a disciple of Feuerbach and it was on this point that Stirner was soon to attack him.

By the end of 1843 the influence of Feuerbach was supreme among all those Young Hegelians who did not attach themselves to Bruno Bauer: Marx, Engels, Hess, Ruge and their associates

[1] L. Feuerbach, op. cit. p. 244.
[2] L. Feuerbach, op. cit. p. 230.
[3] K. Marx, *Frühe Schriften*, i, p. 479.

all shared in the general enthusiasm for the idea of 'man'. The fundamental ambiguity of this entity was to be proved by the splitting up of the movement soon after the publication of the first number of the *Deutsch-französische Jahrbücher*. But as far as Marx was concerned the basis of his second article in that journal 'Kritik der Hegelschen Rechtsphilosophie' was still human emancipation as conceived by Feuerbach. However much it may be doubted whether it is Feuerbach's influence that is paramount in the opening pages on the criticism of religion, there is no doubt that the main themes of humanism, abolition of philosophy and the Franco-German alliance were of Feuerbachian inspiration. Feuerbach's fundamental humanism is plain in the solution that Marx proposes for Germany's difficulties: 'To be radical is to grasp things by the root. But for man the root is man himself . . . the emancipation of Germany will be the emancipation of man'.[1] Marx's advocacy of the abolition of philosophy in order to realise it falls into the pattern of Feuerbach's programme when he demanded that 'man should become the subject matter of philosophy and philosophy itself should be abolished'.[2] My philosophy, he said in an aphorism, is no philosophy. In his 'Thesen' Feuerbach had explained why the intellectual climate of the time required a close co-operation between French and German thinkers. Pursuing as usual his effort to hold the balance between reason and nature, Feuerbach declared that the two essential tools of philosophy are the head, source of activity and idealism, and the heart, source of passivity and feeling. Truth and life were only to be found where 'the sanguine principle of French sense-perception and materialism is united to the phlegm of German metaphysics'.[3] Thus the philosopher who really wished to be in touch with life and mankind would have to be of Gallo-Germanic blood. The heart, the feminine principle and seat of materialism, is French; the head, the masculine principle and seat of idealism, is German. The heart is essential, being the source of all revolution and movement.[4] In his notebooks of that time Feuerbach has the entry: 'What is my principle? Egoism and communism, since both are as inseparable as heart and head. Without egoism you have no head; without com-

[1] Ibid. p. 497.   [2] L. Feuerbach, *Sämtliche Werke*, II, p. 391.
[3] Ibid. p. 235.   [4] Ibid. p. 236.

munism you have no heart'.[1] Marx adopted this parallel of head
and heart and also the necessity of finding a unity, but while
keeping German idealism as the 'head', he looked for a 'heart'
that was other than philosophical to enable him to make the
transition to reality, and found it in the proletariat. He says,
bringing in again the idea of the abolition of philosophy: 'Philosophy is the head of this emancipation [i.e. of man] and the
proletariat is its heart. Philosophy can only be realised by the
abolition of the proletariat and the proletariat can only be
abolished by the realisation of philosophy'.[2]

It was Marx who had most pressingly invited Feuerbach to take
part in the *Deutsch-französische Jahrbücher* by writing a critique
of Schelling as the representative of philosophical idealism. It
seemed to Marx that Feuerbach was the heir to the early thought
of Schelling and thus the ideal man to write this critique:

> You are just the man to do it, because you are the opposite of
> Schelling. The . . . upright thought of Schelling's youth . . .
> has become for you truth, reality, virile force. Thus Schelling
> is your caricature by anticipation . . . so I consider you the
> necessary and natural opponent of Schelling summoned to be
> so by their majesties nature and history. Your struggle with
> him is the struggle of philosophy's imagination with philosophy
> itself.[3]

But Feuerbach, though he continued in close correspondence
with Paris, would not subscribe officially to the review.

It is, however, in the Paris MSS. that Feuerbach is supreme
and his all-pervasive influence cannot escape anyone who care-
fully compares the respective texts. As has been shown above it
was in the 'Thesen' and the 'Grundsätze' that Marx found 'the
only theoretical revolution since Hegel'.[4] This view is confirmed
by a recently published letter of Marx to Feuerbach dated
August 1844 where Marx singles out for praise the 'Grundsätze'
and a smaller article just published, 'Das Wesen des Glaubens im
Sinne Luthers'. He congratulates Feuerbach on having given a

---

[1] L. Feuerbach, *Sämtliche Werke*, ii, p. 391.
[2] K. Marx, *Frühe Schriften*, i, p. 505.
[3] *MEGA*, i, i. 2, pp. 316f.
[4] K. Marx, *Frühe Schriften*, i, p. 508.

philosophical basis to socialism that the communists have been quick to take up and interpret in their own way:

> I am glad to find an opportunity of assuring you of the great admiration and – allow me the word – love that I bear towards you. Your 'Philosophie der Zukunft' and 'Wesen des Glaubens' are in any case, in spite of their limited size, of more weight than all the present-day German literature put together. In these writings you have given – whether intentionally I do not know – a philosophical basis to socialism, and the communists, too, have immediately understood these works in this sense. The unity of man with man, which is based in the real difference between men, the concept of a human species drawn down from the heaven of abstraction to the real earth, what can this be but the concept of society?[1]

Previously, Feuerbach's influence has been attributed almost exclusively to the critique of religion. It is true that in his section on the alienation of labour Marx draws a parallel between the two sorts of alienation: indeed, no less than four times in these few pages Marx refers to religion as a prototype of the alienation he is talking about. But Feuerbach was not the only, and in Marx's eyes probably not the chief, critic of religious alienation. Where Feuerbach was unique was in his anthropology – his picture of man as a being whose essence is communal, whose knowledge comes via sense-perception and who lives in constant interchange with nature. This particularly applies to Marx's sections on 'Private Property and Communism' and his 'Critique of Hegel's Dialectic'.

Anthropology, according to Feuerbach, is the basis of all sciences: 'The new philosophy makes man, together with nature, which is the basis of man, into the unique, universal and highest object of philosophy, that is, it makes anthropology together with physiology into the all-embracing science'.[2] Feuerbach's cult of nature and the senses is reflected in Marx's picture of the 'real, corporeal man with his feet firmly planted on the solid ground, inhaling and exhaling all the powers of nature'.[3] Passion and

[1] L. Feuerbach, *Briefwechsel* (Leipzig, 1963) pp. 183f.

[2] L. Feuerbach, *Sämtliche Werke*, vi, p. 251.

[3] K. Marx, *Frühe Schriften*, i, p. 639.

suffering, too, are qualities of man on which both lay emphasis. For Feuerbach, 'an existence without needs is a superfluous existence . . . a being without suffering is a being without existence'.[1] And Marx: 'To be sentient is to suffer (to experience). Man as an objective sentient being is a suffering being, and, since he feels his suffering, a passionate being'.[2]

Marx's central idea of the humanisation of nature and the naturalisation of man – communism as the 'realised naturalism of man and the realised humanism of nature'[3] – is based on an argument of Feuerbach from *Das Wesen des Christentums*, repeated in the 'Grundsätze', where he says: 'What a being is, can only be known from its object; the object that is necessary to a being is none other than its manifest essence. Thus the object of the eye is light, not sound or smell. The essence of the eye is manifest to us by means of its object'.[4] Again in *Das Wesen des Christentums*: 'Man is nothing without an object. The object that belongs necessarily and essentially to a subject is nothing but the peculiar and objective essence of this subject'.[5] This idea is taken over and elaborated by Marx, being at the root of his conception of the relationship of man and nature. For instance, the following passage from the section on 'Private Property and Communism':

On the one hand, it is only when objective reality everywhere becomes for men in society the reality of human faculties, human reality, and thus the reality of his own faculties, that all objects become for him the objectification of himself. The objects then confirm and realise his individuality, they are his own objects, that is, man himself becomes the object. The manner in which these objects become his own depends upon the nature of the object and the nature of the corresponding faculty; for it is precisely the determinate character of this relation which constitutes the specific real mode of affirmation. The object is not the same for the eye as for the ear, for the ear as for the eye. The distinctive character of each faculty is precisely its characteristic essence and thus also the character-

---

[1] L. Feuerbach, op. cit. II, p. 297. [2] K. Marx, op. cit. p. 651.
[3] K. Marx, op. cit. pp. 593f. [4] L. Feuerbach, op. cit. II, p. 250.
[5] L. Feuerbach, op. cit. VI, p. 5.

istic mode of its objectification, of its objectively real, living being. It is therefore not only in thought, but through all the senses that man is affirmed in the objective world.[1]

This 'man' of Feuerbach and Marx is, according to them, the answer to all the previous contradictions in philosophy which, as good disciples of Hegel, they feel obliged to resolve into some sort of unity. This desire for unity is obvious in Feuerbach's conception of his 'new philosophy' which is 'the negation of both rationalism and mysticism, both pantheism and personalism, both atheism and theism; it is the unity of all these antithetic truths, being itself an absolutely self-sufficient and manifest truth'.[2] This is echoed by Marx's well-known description of communism:

[Communism] is the definite resolution of the antagonism between man and nature, and between man and man. It is the true solution of the conflict between essence and existence, between objectification and self-affirmation, between freedom and necessity, between individual and species. It is the solution of the riddle of history and knows itself to be this solution.[3]

The birth of a new science is predicted by both Feuerbach and Marx to reflect the new situation – a philosophy of man that includes the natural sciences in its scope. Feuerbach says: 'Philosophy must again link itself to natural science, and natural science to philosophy'.[4] This desire for what is united and concrete is made even more emphatic by Marx: 'Sense-experience (see Feuerbach) must be the basis of all science.... Natural science will one day incorporate the science of man, just as the science of man will one day incorporate natural science; there will be a single science'.[5] Feuerbach insists, however, that the community that he is advocating does not involve the loss of any individuality on the part of its members, but rather the contrary: 'The essence of man is only to be found in community, in the unity of man with man – a unity which nevertheless rests on

[1] K. Marx, *Frühe Schriften*, i, pp. 600f.
[2] L. Feuerbach, *Sämtliche Werke*, ii, p. 241.
[3] K. Marx, *Frühe Schriften*, p. 594.
[4] L. Feuerbach, op. cit. p. 244.
[5] K. Marx, op. cit. p. 604.

the reality of the distinction between I and thou'.[1] Marx echoes
this also: 'Individual human life and species-life are not different things. . . . It is just his particularity that makes him an
individual, a real 'individual' communal being'.[2]

Even Marx's view on the relation of theory and practice – 'the
solution of 'theoretical' contradictions themselves is only possible
in a 'practical' way, through the practical energy of man'[3] – is
also an idea of Feuerbach's who said that 'the doubt that theory
will not solve for you will be solved by practice'.[4]

These quotations are enough to show that Marx borrowed a
great deal from Feuerbach when writing the most important
sections of the Paris MSS. The conception of man as a being
whose very essence is modified by his contact with nature and his
fellow men in society, the desire for a radical change based on the
real possibilities offered by this conception (note the prominence
given by both to the word 'positive' which for them means just
that – something real, effective, radical), and the fundamental
unity that Marx thought could thus be achieved – all these are
inspired by his reading of Feuerbach.

In the first work in which Marx and Engels co-operated, *Die
heilige Familie*, written in the latter half of 1844, Marx's admiration for Feuerbach is as strong as ever. The general impression
that the book must have given at the time was that Marx and
Engels were here defending Feuerbach's 'real humanism' against
the attacks of speculative idealists who wanted to put spirit or
self-consciousness in the place of man and his real qualities. The
opening words of *Die heilige Familie* are: 'Real humanism has
no more dangerous enemy in Germany than the spiritualism or
speculative idealism that puts "spirit" or "self-consciousness"
in the place of real, individual man'.[5] Marx himself recognised
this later when in 1867 an admirer sent him a copy of the book
and he re-read it. He wrote to Engels that he was surprised to
find that they did not need to be ashamed of their work 'although
the cult of Feuerbach strikes one as very amusing'.[6]

It is nevertheless important to note that not all the mentions of
Feuerbach in the book are in passages written by Marx. The

[1] L. Feuerbach, op. cit. p. 318.   [2] K. Marx, op. cit. p. 597.
[3] K. Marx, op. cit. p. 602.   [4] L. Feuerbach, op. cit. p. 389.
[5] K. Marx, op. cit. p. 669.   [6] *MEGA*, iii, 3, p. 363.

most enthusiastic was written by Engels, though no doubt with
Marx's approval:

> Who then has discovered the secret of the 'system'? *Feuerbach.*
> Who has destroyed the dialectic of concepts, the war of gods,
> the only one the philosophers knew? *Feuerbach.* Who has put,
> not indeed the 'definition of man' – as though a man could have
> a definition other than that he is a man – but 'man' in place
> of the old rubbish and also in place of 'infinite self-conscious-
> ness'? *Feuerbach and Feuerbach alone.* He has done still
> more. . .'.[1]

The general impression given by *Die heilige Familie* is of a
whole-hearted acceptance and praise of Feuerbach for his achievements in the 'Thesen' and 'Grundsätze', as being the author of
the idea that philosophy was merely an abstract expression of
existing circumstances and the man who 'first described and
investigated philosophy as speculative and mystical empiricism'.[2]
Once again, as in previous writings, the accent is placed on Feuerbach's criticism of Hegel's philosophy, and the only writings of
Feuerbach that are specifically mentioned are the 'Thesen' and
'Grundsätze', in spite of the account of Engels quoted earlier.
In the passage on French materialism Feuerbach's achievement
vis-à-vis Hegel is compared to that of Pierre Bayle *vis-à-vis*
seventeenth-century metaphysics: 'As Feuerbach was driven
from his attack on speculative theology to an attack on speculative philosophy, precisely because he recognised speculation as
the last bulwark of theology . . . so religious doubt drove Bayle to
doubt metaphysics'.[3] This is elaborated a little further on when,
in contrast to Strauss and Bruno Bauer, both of whom remained
inside Hegel's system, Marx says:

> first Feuerbach, who completed and criticised Hegel on Hegel's
> own ground, dissolved the metaphysical absolute spirit into
> 'real man on the basis of nature'. Feuerbach was the first to
> complete the critique of religion in that he sketched out in a
> broad and masterly way a critique of Hegel's speculation and
> thus of all metaphysics.[4]

[1] K. Marx, *Frühe Schriften*, I, p. 776.   [2] Ibid. p. 708.
[3] Ibid. p. 822.   [4] Ibid. p. 838.

From a general point of view the influence of Feuerbach in the
'Grundsätze' appears in two forms:

Firstly it is Feuerbach who helps Marx to formulate the first
version of historical materialism and particularly the idea of a
'basis'. What Feuerbach describes in the general terms of a basis
of 'nature' and a superstructure of 'spirit' becomes in Marx
society and the state – indeed Marx described civil society as the
natural basis of the modern state. The connexion between the
two is seen very clearly in the letter of Marx to Feuerbach quoted
above where Marx asks: 'The unity of man with man that is
based on the real difference between men, the conception of a
human species drawn down from the heaven of abstraction to the
real earth, what can this be but the concept of society?'[1] Inherited, too, from Feuerbach is the ambiguity with regard to
materialism, an ambiguity that was never to be resolved. For on
the one hand Marx describes materialism as 'the teaching of real
humanism and the logical basis of communism' and Feuerbach is
praised for having worked out at a theoretical level a humanism
that was the same as materialism. Yet on the other hand, earlier
in the book, Marx talks, in a phrase that recalls the MSS., about
Feuerbach's overcoming once and for all the old opposition of
idealism and materialism. This repeats the terminology of Feuerbach who in *Das Wesen des Christentums* says: 'Just as man
belongs to the essence of nature, this is a point against vulgar
materialism, so nature belongs to the essence of man – this against
subjective idealism'.[2]

Secondly, so strong is the influence of Feuerbach that Marx
seems in certain passages of *Die heilige Familie* to equate all
notion of a dialectic with idealism and dismiss it as such. Feuerbach's general influence here was very pervasive. Marx wrote to
Engels in 1868 apropos of a book by Eugen Dühring: 'The gentle-
men in Germany believe that Hegel's dialectic is a "dead duck".
Feuerbach has much on his conscience in this respect.'[3] This is
corrected later in the *Deutsche Ideologie* and *Theses* on Feuerbach, where, for example, the idea of a 'natural basis' for society
is criticised in the third thesis: 'The materialistic doctrine con-

---

[1] L. Feuerbach, *Briefwechsel* (Leipzig, 1963) p. 184.

[2] L. Feuerbach, *Sämtliche Werke*, vi, p. 326.

[3] *MEGA*, iii, 4, p. 11.

cerning the changing of circumstances and education forgets that
circumstances are changed by men and that the educator must
himself be educated. This doctrine has therefore to divide society
into two parts, one of which is superior to society'.[1] In the first
part of the *Deutsche Ideologie* Feuerbach's ideas are submitted to
a thorough-going criticism, thus marking the end of his influence
on Marx. Feuerbach's thought did not have enough depth to
have an enduring influence on Marx. But as long as this influence lasted it was extremely important. What was so vital about
Feuerbach's writings was the period in which they were produced.
As Marx said later: 'Compared with Hegel Feuerbach is very
poor. Nevertheless after Hegel he was epoch-making because he
put the emphasis on certain points, uncomfortable for the
Christian consciousness and important for the progress of criticism, which Hegel had left in a sort of mystical twilight between
clarity and obscurity'.

6. DIFFERENCES BETWEEN MARX AND FEUERBACH

In spite of Marx's continuing admiration for Feuerbach, there
were always certain points on which he expressed an adverse
judgement – and that from very early on. His later disagreements
with Feuerbach are foreshadowed in a letter to Ruge written in
March 1843 where he remarks of the 'Thesen': 'The only point
that I do not like about Feuerbach's aphorisms is that he talks
too much about nature and too little about politics. This latter
is the only means by which present philosophy can become a
reality'.[2] But he does not consider this a very serious fault in
Feuerbach for he immediately continues: 'Still, I suppose it will
be like the sixteenth century, when there was a series of enthusi-
asts for the state to balance the nature-worshippers'.[3] What
Feuerbach did say about the state showed that he was certainly
no conservative. 'A people', he said in the 'Thesen', 'who
excludes time from its metaphysics and divinises an eternal, that
is abstract existence separated from time, must also exclude time
from its political affairs and divinise the anti-historical principle of

[1] Marx–Engels, *Werke*, III, p. 533.
[2] *MEGA*, I, i. 2, p. 308.   [3] Ibid.

stability opposed to reason and justice'.[1] Nevertheless the last
but one of the 'Thesen' revealed a view of the state surprisingly
close to that of Hegel:

> Man is the ground of the state. The state is the realised,
> complete and explicit totality of the human essence. In the
> state the essential goals and activities of man are realised in the
> different classes, but again brought to identity in the person of
> the head of state. The head of state has to represent all classes
> without distinction. Before him all are equally necessary
> and have equal rights. The head of state is the representative
> of universal man'.[2]

Marx's general criticism of Feuerbach was that Feuerbach's
doctrines were purely 'contemplative'; they only concerned
themselves with interpretation and thus gave no guide to action.
They seemed to ignore economics and historical development.
Marx believed that this contemplation was not the only means to
knowledge; it had to be supplemented by 'praxis'. Their views
of nature were correspondingly different: for Feuerbach, nature
was what gave immediate truth to the senses, whereas for Marx
nature was no static reality but something constantly changing
itself through the mediation of men. This is Marx's criticism in
the first of his famous *Theses* on Feuerbach:

> The chief defect of all previous materialism (including that of
> Feuerbach) is that things, reality, the sensible world, are con-
> ceived only in the form of objects of observation, but not as
> human sense activity, not as practical activity, not subjectively.
> Hence in opposition to materialism, the active side was de-
> veloped abstractly by idealism, which of course does not know
> real sense activity as such. Feuerbach wants sensible objects
> really distinguished from the objects of thought, but he does
> not understand human activity itself as objective activity. . . .
> He therefore does not grasp the significance of 'revolutionary',
> 'practical-critical' activity'.[3]

This is perhaps not quite just to Feuerbach, for it blames him
for not doing what he never set out to do. Feuerbach certainly

[1] L. Feuerbach, *Sämtliche Werke*, ii, p. 233.　　　[2] Ibid. p. 244.
[3] Marx–Engels, *Werke*, iii, p. 533.

did not underestimate the importance of 'practical activity' as the following quotations from a slightly later work, *Das Wesen der Religion*, written during the troubled year of 1848, show:

> If we not only 'believe' in a better life, but also 'will' it, and will it not in an isolated way, but with our united strength, then we will also 'create' a better life, and at least remove the gross, heart-rending injustices and evils that cry to heaven from which mankind has up till now suffered. [And this can only happen, according to Feuerbach] where an oppressed mass or majority opposes their justified egoism to that of an exclusive nation or caste, where classes or whole nations out of the despised darkness of the proletariat step forward through their victory over the increasing obscurity of a patrician minority into the light of historical celebrity.[1]

But Feuerbach never pursued this line of thought, firstly because the religious problem was the only one that really interested him throughout his life, and secondly he did not judge the situation in Germany in the mid-1840s ripe for a transition from theory to practice – and subsequent events proved him right. Feuerbach was not at all opposed to practical activity at the appropriate time, but he considered it foolish to act before men's minds were sufficiently prepared. Certainly, if we take seriously his preface to the 'Grundsätze' their purpose was practical enough: 'the philosophy of the future has the task of bringing philosophy back again from the realm of "abstract souls" to that of bodily, living souls; from the blessedness of divine and self-sufficient thoughts to the misery of man'.[2] In 1843, when asked to collaborate in the *Deutsch-französische Jahrbücher*, he replied to Ruge:

> From the 'practical' point of view it [that is, a proposed association of French and German radicals] cannot, at the present time, hold together. Quiet influence is the best. First quiet, then loud – not the reverse. Germany can only be cured by poison, not by fire and sword. We have not yet arrived at the point of transition from theory to practice, for we are still

---

[1] L. Feuerbach, *Sämtliche Werke*, VIII, p. 398.

[2] Ibid. II, p. 245.

I

lacking in theory, at least in a complete and fully realised form.[1]

Isolated in his farm at Bruckberg, Feuerbach never took part in the political life of Germany. But his influence via such men as Marx, Engels, Hess, Grün and Ewerbeck, all of whom acknowledged themselves at one time or another as his disciples, was enormous. His importance was thus summed up by Engels in the preface to his *Die Lage der arbeitenden Klassen*: 'More than any other, German socialism and communism had its origin in theoretical presuppositions. Of the avowed representatives of its reforms, there is scarcely a single one that has not come to communism via Feuerbach's dissolution of Hegelian speculation'.[2]

[1] L. Feuerbach, *Briefwechsel*, p. 175.
[2] Marx–Engels, *Werke*, ii, p. 233.

MAX STIRNER

1. STIRNER'S LIFE AND WORKS

MAX STIRNER – whose real name was Kaspar Schmidt – was an only son of Protestant parents, his father being a Bayreuth flute-maker who earned a comfortable living. He died, however, two years after Stirner was born in 1806, his wife remarried a dentist and the family moved to west Prussia. When Stirner was aged twelve he was sent back to Bayreuth and lived there for the next six years while attending the grammar schoool. He went to the University of Berlin at the age of twenty and entered the philo-sophical faculty where he attended, among others, the lectures of Hegel. He stayed there two years, spent the next year at the University of Erlangen and then interrupted his studies to stay at home for some time, possibly owing to the incipient madness of his mother.

By 1832 he was back at the University of Berlin, but two years later he only obtained a limited *facultas docendi* and, when after further studies he failed to get a post in a state school, Stirner started teaching in a private girls' school where he remained until he gave up the job in 1844 just before the publication of his book.

In 1837 Stirner had married the niece of his landlady, but she died a year later in childbirth, and in 1843 Stirner married again, this time Marie Dähnhardt to whom he dedicated *Der Einzige*. She was comparatively wealthy, but the money was lost when the creamery that Stirner had bought with it in 1845 failed the year after, and she left him the same year. Stirner worked as a hack translator of Jean Baptiste Say and Adam Smith, but he was twice imprisoned for debt and died destitute in 1856.

Stirner is a man of a single book, *Der Einzige und sein Eigentum*, and the whole of Stirner's productive period is contained in the years 1842–4. Being a teacher and not immediately connected with the university Stirner did not come into contact with the

Young Hegelians until quite late. What inspired him to his
brief spell of creation was the group of young radical intellectuals
formed in Berlin after Bruno Bauer's dismissal from his post and
known as the *Freien*. They used to meet almost nightly in a wine-
shop belonging to a certain Hippel, and Engels in his comic poem
Der Triumph des Glaubens gives this description of Stirner as he
appeared at these gatherings:

> 'For the time being he is still drinking beer,
> Soon he will drink blood as if it were water;
> As soon as the rest cry savagely "Down with kings!"
> Stirner immediately goes the whole hog: "Down with
> laws too!"' '

Stirner cannot have joined the group before the end of 1841 as
this was the time that Marx, who apparently never met Stirner,
left Berlin. During this period Stirner wrote several short articles
for newspapers, among which a very laudatory review of Bruno
Bauer's *Posaune*, and also two longer articles published in the
supplement to the *Rheinische Zeitung*, one on education as the
development of the self and the second, in which the influence of
Feuerbach is evident, on the very Hegelian subject of the relation
between art and religion. Stirner also published two articles a
little later in the *Berliner Monatsschrift*, a review edited by one of
the *Freien*, the first rejecting any ideas of the state, while in the
second, a commentary of Eugène Sue's popular novel *Les
Mystères de Paris*, Stirner elevates the self at the expense of any
fixed moral norms.

Stirner spent most of 1843 writing *Der Einzige und sein
Eigentum*. It was finished by April 1844 and published in
November of that year. For all its apparent eccentricities the
book is very obviously a product of its time and of the Young
Hegelian movement in particular. The form of the book, dialectical and divided into triads, is Hegelian, as is also the careful
attention paid to language and the roots of words. Inside the
Young Hegelian movement itself, Stirner carried to an extreme
their rejection of anything religious and their opposition to any
'system'. The familiar accusation of still thinking in a 'theological' manner, that is in an abstract manner which still left some
ideas or principles outside, and in some way opposed to, the minds

of men, and the accusation of lack of consequence and perseverance in drawing the full conclusion from premises both reach their culmination in Stirner who sees all his fellow-thinkers as 'spiritual' and 'religious' as compared to himself.

Stirner can thus be seen as the last of the Hegelians, last perhaps because he was the most logical, not attempting to replace Hegel's 'concrete universal' by any 'humanity' or 'classless' society since he had no universal, only the individual, all-powerful ego. Stirner took Hegel's views as his basis and then worked out his own philosophy by criticising everything that was positive in Hegel's critics, Bauer, Feuerbach and Marx – whose criticisms, according to Stirner, were never pushed far enough. Hegelianism was thus at an end: Stirner only used the form not the content of the Hegelian system and, like all the Young Hegelians, was most fascinated by the dialectic. But even this was only an outer shell, for Stirner was very weak on history as he had no room to allow for a historical development whether of the world spirit, self-consciousness or the class struggle. Stirner was indeed a solipsist and a nihilist but, for all his criticism of Feuerbach, he was still influenced by his naturalistic viewpoint. For Stirner's individualism left no room for any sort of morality, which had been on the side of freedom in Hegel. Since the ethical sphere was left empty it is not surprising that Stirner sometimes lapsed into a Feuerbachian naturalism based on natural values and needs.

Stirner's book is a difficult one because there is no rectilinear development and it often presents the appearance of notes taken at random and put down with no attempt at co-ordination. For example, at the beginning of the book we are offered two entirely different schemata of world history. Also Stirner's attitude to Bruno Bauer changes considerably in the course of the book, but no attempt is made to reconcile the two views. Indeed, what Stirner himself says on this point probably applies to most of the book: 'The foregoing review of "free human criticism" was written bit by bit immediately after the appearance of the books in question, as was also that which elsewhere refers to the writings of this tendency, and I did little more than bring together the fragments'.[1] The development is nevertheless progressive as the same points are returned to later and treated at

[1] M. Stirner, *The Ego and His Own*, p. 190.

greater length. A second factor complicating Stirner's exposition
is his treatment of language. He tries continually to obtain new
effects by translating foreign words into German, by giving their
original meaning to words in current use and by etymological
investigations into the roots of words. Of course, all this makes
translation difficult.

The basic message of the book, as well as the style in which it is
written, is best shown by quoting the first and last paragraphs of
the preface:

> What is not supposed to be my concern? First and foremost
> the good cause, then God's cause, then the cause of mankind,
> of truth, freedom, humanity, justice . . . finally, even the cause
> of mind and a thousand other causes. Only *my* cause is never
> to be my concern. Shame on the egoist who thinks only of
> himself.[1]

And the last paragraph reads:

> The divine is God's concern; the human, man's. My concern
> is neither the divine nor the human, not the good, true, just,
> free, etc., but solely what is *mine*, and it is not a general one, but
> is – *unique*, as I am unique.[2]

The layout of the book is clearly modelled on Feuerbach's *Das
Wesen des Christentums*, being divided into two parts entitled
'man' and 'myself', which correspond to the two parts of Feuerbach's work that dealt respectively with God and man. The first
chapter of *Der Einzige* describes a human life in a triadic form:

> The child was realistic, taken up with the things of this world,
> till little by little he succeeded in getting at what was at the
> back of these things; the youth was idealistic, inspired by
> thoughts, till the stage where he became the man, the egoistic
> man who deals with things and thoughts according to his heart's
> pleasure, and sets his personal interest above everything.
> Finally the old man? 'When I become one, there will be time
> enough to speak of that'.[3]

Stirner then goes on to apply this to human history: antiquity

[1] Ibid. p. 3.   [2] Ibid. p. 6.
[3] M. Stirner, *The Ego and His Own*, p. 16.

was the childhood of the human race, the modern age its adolescence and its maturity will be that immediate future of which Stirner's book is a precursor. The view of history as a gradual progress of philosophical thought is Hegelian, but in place of the reign of spirit, Stirner puts the supremacy of the self and its property. His analysis of the modern age is a sort of demonology of the spirits to which humanity has been successively enslaved.

Since Stirner's ideas can best be understood by comparing them with those of his contemporaries, the most revealing part of the book is his attitude to his fellow Young Hegelians. After dealing with antiquity, in which nature and her laws were regarded as a reality more powerful than man, Stirner describes at greater length the modern, the Christian world, the kingdom of pure spirituality, whether in religion or philosophy, the latest manifestation of which – the philosophy of Feuerbach – is still 'throughly theological'.

According to Stirner, Feuerbach has merely changed the Christian conception of grace into his idea of a human species and religious commands into moral ones. But the Christian dualism between what is essential and what is non-essential in man remains; indeed, the situation is even worse than before for this dualism, since it has been brought down from heaven to earth, has thereby become even more inescapable: if Feuerbach destroys the heavenly dwelling of the 'spirit of God' and forces it to move to earth bag and baggage, then we, its earthly apartments, will be badly overcrowded. 'Feuerbach', says Stirner, 'thinks that if he humanises the divine he has found the truth. No; if God has given us pain, "man" is capable of pinching us still more torturingly'.[1] Men are still bound by ideals that stand above and separate from them. The humanist religion of Feuerbach is only the last metamorphosis of the Christian religion: 'Now that liberalism has proclaimed "man" we can now declare openly that herewith was only completed the consistent carrying out of Christianity and that in truth Christianity set itself no other task from the start than to realise "man", the "true" man'.[2] The only solution is therefore to do away with the divinity once and for all in any shape or form: 'Can the man-God really die if only the God in him dies?'[3] For a genuine liberation, we must not only

[1] Ibid. p. 227.   [2] Ibid. p. 228.   [3] Ibid. p. 202.

kill God, but man, too. Stirner here, in a typically Young Hegelian manner, takes up Feuerbach's own starting point and turns it against its author who is accused of not having followed it through to its proper end. All philosophy for Stirner, as for Marx too, was idealism, but whereas for Marx the basis to which philosophy had to be reduced was socio-economic, for Stirner it was the ego.

Stirner now goes on to deal with the 'most modern among the moderns' – the *Freien* or Liberals, whom he divides into three classes: political, social and humane.

Stirner begins the first section with a characterisation of the changes that came over the political scene in the eighteenth century:

> After the chalice of the so-called monarchy had been drained down to the dregs, in the eighteenth century people became aware that their drink did not taste human – too clearly aware not to begin to crave a different cup. Since our fathers were human beings after all, they at last desired also to be regarded as such.[1]

The new idea that gained ground at this time was that 'in our being together as a nation or state we are human beings. How we act in other respects as individuals and what self-seeking impulses we may there succumb to, belongs solely to our private life; our public or state life is a purely human one'.[2] The bourgeoisie developed itself in the struggle against the privileged classes by whom it was cavalierly treated as the third estate and confounded with the *canaille*. But now that the idea of the quality of man spread, the situation, as with Feuerbach's critique of religion, became much worse. For just as Feuerbach, by transferring the centre of religion from heaven to earth, had rendered its effects more immediate and obvious, so democracy renders more obvious the evils of politics. Stirner quotes Mirabeau's exclamation: 'Is not the people the source of all *power*?' He goes on: 'The monarch in the person of the "royal master" had been a paltry monarch compared with this new one, the "sovereign nation". This monarchy was a thousand times stricter, severer and more consistent.'[3] This liberation, the second phase of protestantism,

[1] Ibid. p. 128.   [2] Ibid. p. 128.   [3] Ibid. p. 132.

was inaugurated by the bourgeoisie and its watchword was rationalism. But this merely means the independence of persons, liberalism for the liberals and a replacing of personal power by one that is impersonal. It is no longer any individual, but the state itself and its laws that are the despots. Laws and decrees multiply and all thought and action become regulated. In return for this slavery the liberal state guarantees our life and property, but this free competition means merely that everyone can push forward, assert himself and fight one against another. The bourgeoisie also has a morality closely bound up with its essence, one that emphasises solid business, honourable trade and a moral life, disregarding all the time that the practice of this rests on the foundation of the exploitation of labour.

Under the heading of 'Social Liberalism' Stirner next deals with the doctrines of the communists. Whereas through the Revolution the bourgeoisie had become omnipotent and everyone was raised (or degraded) to the dignity of 'citizen', communism or social liberalism responds:

> Our dignity and essence consist not in our being all equal children of our mother, the state, but in our all existing each for the other ... that each exists only through the other who, while caring for my wants, at the same time sees his own satisfied by me. It is labour that constitutes our dignity and our equality.[1]

Stirner's summary of the socialist doctrine is: all must have nothing, so that all may have. Under liberalism it is what he 'has' that makes the man and in 'having' people are unequal. But this society where we are all to become members of the *Lumpenproletariat* is even worse than the previous ones, for here 'neither command nor property is left to the individual; the state took the former, society the latter'.[2] The communist ideas show the same faults as those already criticised. They, too, have a dualistic view of man:

> That the communist sees in you the man, the brother, is only the Sunday side of communism. According to the workday side he does not take you as man simply, but as human labourer or labouring man. The first view has in it the liberal principle;

[1] M. Stirner, *The Ego and His Own*, p. 156. [2] Ibid. p. 155.

in the second illiberality is concealed. If you were lazy, he would certainly not fail to recognise the man in you, but would endeavour to cleanse him as a 'lazy man' from laziness and to convert him to the 'faith' that labour is man's destiny and calling'.[1]

Thus in the communists' glorification of society we merely have another in the line of deities that have tyrannised over mankind: 'Society, which is the source of all we have, is a new master, a new spook, a new "supreme being", which "takes us into its service and allegiance".'[2]

The criticism of communism advanced by the humanist liberal, or disciple of Bruno Bauer, to whom Stirner next passes, is that if society prescribes to the individual his work, then even this does not necessarily make it a purely human activity. For to be this it must be the work of a 'man' and that requires that he who labours should know the human object of his labour and he can have this consciousness only when he knows himself as man, the crucial condition is self-consciousness – the very watchword of Bruno Bauer and his School. 'Humanist liberalism says: "You want labour; all right, we want it likewise, but we want it in the fullest measure. We want it, not that we may gain spare time, but that we may find all satisfaction in labour itself. We want labour because it is our self-development".'[3] In short, man can only be truly himself in human, self-conscious labour. According to Stirner this view seems to say that one cannot be more than man. He would sooner say that one cannot be less: 'It is not man that makes up your greatness, but you create it, because you are more than man and mightier than other – men'.[4] Stirner concedes that among social theories, Bauer's ideas are certainly the most complete for they remove everything that separates man from man. It is in Bauer's criticism, reminiscent of Feuerbach, that Stirner finds the 'purest fulfilment of the love principle of Christianity, the true social principle', which he rejects with the question: 'How can you be truly single so long as even one connection exists between you and other men?'[5] These are the same objections as Stirner

[1] Ibid. p. 160.   [2] Ibid. p. 162.
[3] M. Stirner, *The Ego and His Own*, p. 173.
[4] Ibid. p. 176.   [5] Ibid. p. 177.

brought against Feuerbach. For Bauer shares Feuerbach's humanism and sacrifices the individual man to the idea of humanity by maintaining that his vocation is to realise the human essence through the development of free self-consciousness.

Nevertheless, Stirner does admire Bruno Bauer with his extreme dialectic and proclamation of the perpetual dissolution of ideas. In fact, Stirner thinks that this must finally end up in his own position:

> It is precisely the keenest critic who is hit the hardest by the curse of his principle. Putting from him one exclusive thing after another ... at last, when all ties are undone, he stands alone. He, of all men, must exclude anything that has anything exclusive or private; and when you get to the bottom, what can be more exclusive than the exclusive, unique person himself?[1]

Bauer does, indeed, in later numbers of his *Allgemeine Literatur-Zeitung* reject this Feuerbachian humanism in favour of a 'pure criticism', and Stirner adds to this section a postscript in which he deals with Bauer's change of position as not going nearly far enough:

> [Bauer] is saying too much when he speaks of 'criticising criticism itself'. It, or rather he, has only criticised its oversight and cleared it of its inconsistencies. If he really wanted to criticise criticism he would have to look and see whether there was anything in its pre-supposition.[2]

It still remains true that Stirner found himself closer in outlook to Bauer than to any other of the Young Hegelians and this feeling was reciprocated: Bauer was the only one, apart from Buhl, to attend Stirner's funeral and pay him this last mark of respect.

After thus dismissing the wiles of religion, philosophy and liberalism in their efforts to subdue the self, Stirner shows in the second part of the book the way to its complete liberation. It is not through attachment to other eternal ideas or values that the self is liberated, but by elevating itself above all the toils and snares of these ideas. My self is my own creation and my own property, its power is without limits and it belongs wholly to me. It is only

[1] Ibid. p. 177f.   [2] Ibid. p. 199.

in my own self that this liberation can be found, as Stirner points out, again in opposton to Feuerbach:

> Feuerbach in his 'Grundsätze' is always harping on 'being'. In this he, too, for all his antagonism to Hegel and the absolute philosophy, is stuck fast in abstraction; for 'being' is an abstraction as is also 'the I'. Only I am not an abstraction: I am all in all, consequently even abstraction or nothing; I am not a mere thought, but at the same time I am full of thoughts, a thought-world.[1]

This is a complete inversion of Hegel. What in Hegel was attributed to the general is here applied to the individual. Stirner, too, could have claimed to have stood Hegel on his head. Later Stirner explicitly compares the ego to God, whom 'names cannot name'. But this liberty needs to be supplemented by property. The only thing that really belongs to me is my self: this, too, is the only thing that is really free. Any lesser freedom is really useless, for it always carries with it the implication of a future enslavement, as Stirner has shown in dealing with the different liberal doctrines. The only reason that men do not grasp their liberty is that they have been taught to mistrust themselves and depend on priests, parents or law-givers. But if they are sincere with themselves they will admit that even so their actions are governed by self-love. Dare therefore to free yourself from all that is not your self. In place of 'deny yourself' the slogan of the egoist is 'return to yourself'. In the past people have been shame-faced egoists, now they should come out into the open and grasp for themselves what before they thought to acquire by persuasion, prayer and hypocrisy. Liberty is not something that can be granted – it has to be seized.

The liberal state sees me simply as a member of the human race and it does not interest itself in my peculiarities: it merely demands that I subordinate my individual interests to those of society in general. But human society and the rights of Man mean nothing to me: I seem to have many similarities with my fellows, but at the bottom I am incomparable. My flesh is not their flesh and my mind is not their mind. I refuse to forget myself for the benefit of others. Others – nations, society, state – are nothing but a means which I use. I convert them into my

---

[1] M. Stirner, *The Ego and His Own*, p. 453.

property and my creatures, I put in their place the association of egoists, that is to say, an association of selves of flesh and blood preferring themselves to everything else and having no inclination to sacrifice themselves to this species-man that is the ideal of liberalism. This species-man is plainly nothing but a concept, an idea, a ghost: the true self is without species, without norm, without model, without laws, without duty, without rights.

Law, too, is something that is offered me from the outside. But I am sole judge of what my rights are: they are co-terminous with my 'power', for 'only "your might", "your power", gives you the right'.[1] The only thing that I have not got the right to do is what I have not authorised myself. The only law for me is that which exists in and through my self.

The worst enemy of the self is thus the state, for it is continually opposed to the will of particular persons: I can never alienate my will from the state, as my will is something continually changing. Even the best type of state is one where I am a slave to myself. Did I but realise it, my will is something that no force can break. This does not mean, however, that there will be complete chaos and each man will be able to do as he pleases. For if all men act as egoists and defend themselves, then nothing untoward will happen to them. Marx's view was too cosmopolitan for Stirner whose one passion was the individual person. Stirner considered that it was no use bettering the universal, the state, law, society. Progress was inductive, from below, from individuals. Although he shared with Marx the same criticisms of the Prussian state, the principles upon which these were based were different: Marx was a violent critic of any kind of atomism, from Epicurus's onwards. Stirner on the other hand wanted the state to dissolve into atoms.

The liberal state's aim is to guarantee a little piece of property to everyone. But in fact property falls a prey to the big owners and the proletariat increases and the attacks of the communists are justified. Stirner's criticism of the liberal state here was quite probably influenced by Marx's article 'Zur Judenfrage'; both have the same views on the dualism of the private and political spheres, the difference between corporations and free competition, and the essential features of the Christian state. The solution lies in the formation of an association of people who remain their

[1] Ibid. p. 254.

particular selves, an association which would dispossess the proprietors and organise their wealth in common, each man bringing as much as he can conquer. By all means have associations to reduce the amount of labour needed but let the self and its unique power always have first priority. The supreme law quoted at all those who try to free themselves is that of love: 'every man must have something that is more to him than himself'. This love is not to be a free gift, but is an injunction laid upon us. Certainly I may sacrifice all sorts of things for others, but I cannot sacrifice myself. The egoist loves others because this love makes him happy and has its basis in his egoism.

As an egoist I enjoy all those possessions that my liberation has granted me; they are my property and I dispose of them as I wish. I am even master of my ideas and change them as so many suits of clothes. But this does not mean that I am solitary and isolated. For man is by nature social. Family, friends, political party, state, all these are natural associations, so many chains that the egoist breaks in order to form a 'free association' supple and changeable according to varying interests.

Stirner admits that this 'association of egoists' must be based on a principle of love, but it is an egoistic love – *my* love. The association is my own creation and I enter and leave when I please. I am the only person who attaches myself to the association.

The aim of the association is not revolution, but revolt, not to create new institutions, but to institute themselves. Stirner realised the self-contradictory notion of his 'association of egoists' and in his replies to the critics of his book the element of association is minimised. The book ends, as it began, with an assertion of the uniqueness of the individual:

I am the *owner* of my might, and I am so when I know myself as *unique*. In the *unique one* the owner himself returns into his creative void out of which he was born. Every higher essence above me, be it God, be it man, weakens the feeling of my uniqueness and pales only before the sun of my consciousness of this fact. If I concern myself with myself, the unique one, then my concern is limited to its transitory, mortal creator which constitutes myself, and I can say: All things are nothing to me![1]

[1] M. Stirner, *The Ego and His Own*, p. 496.

2. STIRNER VERSUS FEUERBACH

Unlike Bruno Bauer, Feuerbach and Hess, Stirner had no positive doctrine to offer Marx: but he nevertheless played a very important role in the development of Marx's thought by detaching him from the influence of Feuerbach. This role of Stirner in detaching Marx from Feuerbach can best be made clear by showing firstly that Marx at the time of the publication of *Der Einzige und sein Eigentum* was, and (more important) was regarded as being, a disciple of Feuerbach, secondly that Stirner's book was regarded as important and that his criticism of Feuerbach had wide influence and thirdly that the *Deutsche Ideologie* was composed in the context of this debate and comprises a criticism of Feuerbach which borrows elements from Stirner and a criticism of Stirner which tacitly admits the validity of his attack on Feuerbach but maintains that it no longer applies.

As regards the first point, there are many facts showing that Marx was regarded in late 1844 as being a disciple of Feuerbach. This was certainly so in the eyes of Stirner: the only reference to Marx in *Der Einzige* is to his use of the term *Gattungswesen* in his essay 'Zur Judenfrage', and this term is one borrowed from Feuerbach (first chapter of *Das Wesen des Christentums*).

Feuerbach is referred to as a communist in *Der Einzige*.[1] The use of this word was at that time very loose and many did not distinguish it from socialism, but when in 1843 the Young Hegelian movement split, Feuerbach, at the height of his influence then and in the subsequent year, came to be regarded as the inspirer of the materialist wing in the same way as Bruno Bauer of the idealists.

In 1845 there appeared an article by G. Julius, former editor of the *Leipziger Allgemeine Zeitung* and friend of Bruno Bauer, entitled 'Kritik der Kritik der kritischen Kritik', in which Marx is treated simply as a disciple of Feuerbach. 'In his construction of human nature', says Julius 'Marx by no means does away with dualism: all he does is to transpose this dualism into the real material world in which he follows Feuerbach exactly'.

Bruno Bauer, too, in his reply to Stirner, entitled 'Charakteristik Feuerbachs', tries to show that Stirner is a refutation of Feuer-

[1] Ibid. p. 412.

bachianism as expounded by his disciples Marx, Engels and Hess, but that both are dogmatisms which must in turn be overcome by 'pure criticism'.

Hess, in particular in his essays in *21 Bogen aus der Schweiz*, made great use of the Feuerbachian idea of alienation and viewed his 'true socialism' as the realisation of Feuerbach's philosophy: and Marx and Engels were at this time closely associated with Hess.

At the time of the appearance of Stirner's book Marx had only published, apart from the two essays in '*Anekdota*' and some articles in the *Rheinische Zeitung*, the essays in the *Deutsch-französische Jahrbücher* which are plainly under the influence of Feuerbach.

Finally, there is the evidence of Marx himself, his high praise of Feuerbach in the *Heilige Familie*, written before the appearance of *Der Einzige*, where Marx attributes to Feuerbach alone the overturning of the old system and the placing of 'man' in the centre of philosophical discussion.

As to the second point, that is, the importance of *Der Einzige* at the time and its criticism of Feuerbach: each of the groups attacked by Stirner replied at considerable length, Szeliga and Bruno Bauer both wrote articles, Feuerbach also replied. Hess wrote an essay 'Die letzten Philosophen', Marx and Engels wrote the best part of a book. Even as late as 1847–8 the young Kuno Fischer devoted his first publications to an attack on *Der Einzige*.

All acknowledged that Stirner was an adversary of note. Bruno Bauer wrote in his article that Stirner was 'the most capable and courageous of all the combatants' (that is of his 'pure criticism'). Feuerbach in a letter described Stirner as 'the most gifted and the freest writer it has been given me to meet'. Even Engels in his first letter to Marx discussing the book (19 November 1844) wrote that 'among the *Freien* it is plain that Stirner has the most talent, personality and energy'.

In view of this evidence, the fact that the book was very much a product of its time and that its interest has therefore largely disappeared should not obscure its great importance for its contemporaries.

The most influential part of the book was its criticism of Feuerbach on the grounds that his notion of 'man' was only yet one more universal abstraction to which men would be as enslaved as before. Indeed it was worse than the previous ones since they were at least idealistic and heavenly: now the tyranny had been brought down to earth and would thus be the more difficult to escape. Feuerbach had achieved the 'final metamorphosis of Christianity'.[1]

Ruge, at least, considered the book a decisive criticism of socialism. In a letter to Nauwerck he described the book as a liberation from the 'social dogmatism of artisans' and in a letter to Hess he refuses Hess's request for collaboration on the grounds that Stirner has destroyed Hess's philosophical communism.

Finally, the only reason for Marx and Engels devoting such a large part (three-quarters) of the *Deutsche Ideologie* to a criticism of Stirner was that Stirner was considered by them as the most dangerous enemy of socialism at that time. There can have been nothing personal: it is very improbable that Marx ever met Stirner. The fact that the book was never published is, though not surprising, immaterial: Marx and Engels tried very hard to find a publisher.

As to the third point, that is, the treatment of Feuerbach and Stirner in the *Deutsche Ideologie*, Marx and Engels clearly separate themselves from Feuerbach in a way they had never done before, thereby implicitly accepting the criticism of Stirner. What is criticised in Feuerbach is his *Sinnlichkeit*, his static materialism. This is an aspect of Feuerbach's thought which only came to the fore in his reply to Stirner, as a means of defending himself against the charge of abstraction. To this Marx and Engels oppose their notion of 'praxis', best expressed in the first thesis on Feuerbach: 'The chief defect of all previous materialism (including that of Feuerbach) is that things, reality, the sensible world, are conceived only in the form of objects of observation, but not as human sense activity, not as practical activity (praxis), not subjectively'.[2] Given the circumstances in which the *Deutsche Ideologie* was written, it is impossible that Stirner not only compelled Marx to revise his position *vis-à-vis* Feuerbach but also contributed something to this revision through the idea of the 'creative ego'

[1] M. Stirner, *The Ego and His Own*, p. 229.
[2] Marx–Engels, *Werke*, III, p. 533.

K

that he opposed to all abstractions. Certainly Stirner seems to
have been in Marx's mind when he was composing the section on
Feuerbach in the *Deutsche Ideologie*. There are many references
to Stirner and even a parody of him in the well-known description
of the future communist society:

> In communist society, where no one has an exclusive sphere of
> activity, but can perfect himself in any branch that pleases
> him, society regulates general production and thus makes it
> possible for me to do one thing today and another tomorrow,
> hunt in the morning, fish in the afternoon, raise cattle in the
> evening and go in for criticism after dinner, as I please, without
> ever becoming either hunter, fisherman or critic.[1]

The first unfavourable reference to Proudhon in Marx's
writings appears in the *Deutsche Ideologie*, obviously in connection
with Stirner's recent attack:

> We invite St Sancho [Max Stirner] to show us, for example, in
> Owen (who, as representative of English communism can just as
> well count for 'communism' as Proudhon, who is not a com-
> munist and from whose writings he has extracted most of the
> above phrases) a passage that contains something of the above
> phrases on 'essence', general organisation of work, etc.[2]

Just as it seems clear that this coolness towards Proudhon is a
result of Stirner's criticism (though never acknowledged), so to
some extent in the case of Feuerbach. It is also likely that Marx's
constant attacks on anything that appeared to be based on
'morality' or 'love' in true socialism was due to Stirner's ruthless
criticism of all such notions.

3. Stirner and Marx

It seems doubtful whether any 'direct influence' of Stirner on
Marx in economic matters is provable. This can be seen from an
examination of the dates: the principal work of Marx on alienated labour 'as such' is the MSS. written in Paris in 1844. There
is nothing new on alienated labour in the *Heilige Familie* and in

------

[1] Ibid. p. 33.   [2] Ibid. p. 197.

the *Deutsche Ideologie*, and though the analysis of 1844 is repeated, it is only done so *en passant* and much more attention is
paid to the historical side – its origin in the division of labour.
Stirner's book was published about September 1844, certainly no
earlier than August, the month by which the Paris MSS. of Marx
were completed. So what this parallelism will show is that Marx
was by no means the only person to be thinking of such things at
this time.

Marx's theory as set out in the Paris MSS.[1] can be briefly
summarised as follows:

1. The product of man is not his own but turns into a hostile
   power that dominates him.
2. The act by which man produces is not free but forced.
3. Man's relation to nature is vitiated and he can no longer
   appropriate it as he should.
4. His relation to his fellow-men is also vitiated since he must
   be in a state of subjection *vis-à-vis* his employer.

This idea is briefly anticipated in Marx's essay 'Zur Judenfrage', but only with regard to money, and not products. He
says: 'Under the sway of egoistic need man can only affirm
himself and produce objects in practice by subordinating his products and his own activity to the domination of an alien entity,
and by attributing to them the significance of an alien entity,
namely money'.

What this involves can be seen more clearly by looking at
Marx's ideas of what labour in an unalienated society would look
like. In his notebooks Marx drafted out a few comments on the
economists he was reading at the same time as the writing of the
Paris MSS. The comment on James Mill contains a very interesting passage where Marx deals with what he called 'free labour',
whose preconditions were:

1. that my production should be an objectification of my own
   individuality.
2. that my product should satisfy the needs of others, as, for
   instance, a composer and the singer of his song [My example,
   not Marx's].

[1] *MEGA*, i, 3, pp. 29ff.

3. that my product should mediate between you and the species, should be a completion of your essence, should be known and felt by you to be a necessary part of yourself and that therefore I should feel myself confirmed in my thought and in my feelings;

4. that in my exterior activity I should have created your exterior activity and thus have confirmed my common human essence. Given these conditions, says Marx, our products would be like mirrors in which we could see reflected our common essence.

Coupled with the section on Feuerbach in the *Deutsche Ideologie* is a long and wearisome attack on Stirner enlivened by only occasional bright spots, the sum of which is that Stirner is criticising a communism that no longer exists and never did exist. This latter at least is not true (see the essays of Hess in *21 Bogen aus der Schweiz* and of Marx in *Deutsch-französische Jahrbücher*). It is worth while noting, too, that the writings referred to as a refutation of Stirner's attack on 'essence' in Proudhon are not those of Marx or Hess, but those of Owen. Though it is certainly true that the ideas in the *Deutsche Ideologie* are different from those criticised by Stirner, it is reasonable to suppose that these differences are, to a considerable extent, due precisely to that criticism.

The principal reason for this neglect of Stirner when treating of the development of Marx's thought is that Feuerbach is regarded as the last influence on Marx before the formulation of historical materialism in the *Deutsche Ideologie*. This misconception was started by Engels in his lucidly, too lucidly, written brochure *Ludwig Feuerbach und der Ausgang der klassischen deutschen Philosophie* (1886). Here Feuerbach is separated from the list of the Young Hegelians, Strauss, Bauer, Stirner, and treated afterwards, thus giving the impression that this was the chronological order. This is belied by the dates themselves: Feuerbach's last significant contribution to the Young Hegelian debate was 'Grundsätze der Philosophie der Zukunft', published in July 1843, whereas *Der Einzige* appeared late 1844. This mistake has persisted even in very recent books none of which[1]

[1] With the exception of H. Arvon, *Aux sources de l'existentialisme, Max Stirner*.

give any place at all to the influence of Stirner and also treat the contribution of Feuerbach as coming after Stirner.[1]

It has been seen quite rightly that the 'Feuerbach' part of the *Deutsche Ideologie* brings this period of Marx's writings to a close, but what has not been seen is that it was the following and larger part entitled 'Sankt Max' that both compelled and enabled this culmination. The 'Sankt Max' may be too turgid to be worth while reading but it *is* worth while asking why it is there at all.

Stirner's economic ideas are not clearly formulated (in keeping with the style of the book) but still many parallels to Marx are obvious.[2] These are chiefly found in the sections on political and social liberalism.[3] In the former there is a passage on the omnipotence of money that is closely parallel to the passage in the Paris MSS. where Marx quotes Shakespeare (Timon of Athens) and remarks: 'What I as a man am unable to do, and thus what all my individual faculties are unable to do, is made possible for me by money.... In mediating thus money is a genuinely creative power'.

The passage in Stirner reads: ' "Money governs the world" is the keynote of the bourgeois epoch. A destitute aristocrat and a destitute labourer amount to nothing so far as political significance is concerned. Birth and labour do not do it, but money brings consideration (*Das Geld gibt Geltung*)'.[4]

One place where Stirner seems to anticipate Marx is where he briefly mentions a doctrine which Marx will later make into one of the corner-stones of his economic theory – the doctrine of surplus value. Stirner says:

Under the regime of the commonalty (*Bürgertum*) the labourers always fall into the hands of the possessors – that is of those who have at their disposal some bit of the state domains,

[1] See S. Hook, *From Hegel to Marx*, M. Friedrich, *Philosophie u. Okonomie beim jungen Marx*. R. Tucker has managed to write a whole book on *Philosophy and Myth in Karl Marx* without once mentioning Stirner.

[2] These are hinted at but not gone into in the book by D. Koigen *Zur Vorgeschichte des modernen deutschen Sozialismus* (Bern, 1901).

[3] M. Stirner, *The Ego and His Own*, pp. 128 ff., 152 ff.

[4] Ibid. p. 150.

especially money and land – of the capitalists therefore. The labourer cannot realise on his labour to the extent of the value that it has for the consumer. The capitalist has the greatest profit from it.

In the section on social liberalism (i.e. communism) Stirner has a passage analysing the bad effects of division of labour and the workers' deprivation of their products which is very like what Marx was writing at the same time:

> When everyone is to cultivate himself into man, condemning a man to machine-like labour amounts to the same thing as slavery. If a factory worker must tire himself to death twelve hours or more, he is cut off from becoming man. Every labour is to have the intent that man be satisfied. Therefore he must become a master in it, too, that is be able to perform it as a totality. He who in a pin-factory only puts on the heads, only draws the wire, etc., works, as it were, mechanically, like a machine; he remains half-trained, does not become a master: his labour cannot satisfy him, by itself, has no object in itself, is nothing complete in itself; he labours only into another's hands and is used (exploited) by this other.[1]

Even the call of the Eleventh Feuerbach Thesis 'to change the world' finds its echo here:

> When, for example, a branch of industry is ruined and thousands of labourers become breadless, people think reasonably enough to acknowledge that it is not the individual who must bear the blame, but that 'the evil lies in the situation'.
>
> Let us change the situation, then, but let us change it thoroughly, so that its fortuity becomes powerless.[2]

It is difficult to show any direct influence of Stirner on Marx here, the more so as Stirner's book was to a large extent an amalgam of current clichés. What the above passages show is that the ideas of alienated labour and exploitation were by no means confined to Marx at this time, even among Germans. Both Stirner and Marx were probably much influenced by the ideas of Fourier.

[1] Ibid. pp. 157.   [2] Ibid. pp. 158f.

MOSES HESS

1. EARLY LIFE AND FIRST BOOK:
'DIE HEILIGE GESCHICHTE DER MENSCHHEIT'

MOSES HESS was born in 1812 in Bonn in the Rhineland, the eldest son among five children. The family were strict Jews. His father was a business man who set up a sugar refinery in Cologne in 1816, leaving Moses under the care of his grandfather, a remarkable man who seems to have left an indelible influence on him that Hess later described as follows:

> My extremely orthodox grandfather was a man very learned in the Scriptures who had the title and knowledge of a rabbi without making a profession of it. Every day of the year when he had finished his business he would study the Talmud with its many commentaries until past midnight. This study was only interrupted during the 'nine days'. He used to read then the stories of the Jews' expulsion from Israel to his grandsons, who had to stay up with him until after midnight. The strict old man's snow-white beard would be drenched with tears at this reading; we children, too, of course, could not prevent ourselves from weeping and sobbing.[1]

Hess's mother died when he was fourteen and his father took him to Cologne and made him enter the family business. Hess, however, used his free time to read Spinoza and Rousseau and, not having the temperament to submit to this sort of apprenticeship, came into inevitable conflict with his father and left home in 1833.

Hess went to Holland and France, where no doubt he acquired a certain knowledge of socialist writings and teachings. However, need eventually drove him home, a reconciliation was arrived at with his father and he once again went to work in the family

[1] M. Hess, *Rom und Jerusalem*, 2nd ed. (Leipzig, 1899) p. 16.

business. In his free time he attended a few lectures at Bonn, but
he was essentially a self-taught man and continued reading widely
on his own. The result of these early researches was his first book
Die heilige Geschichte der Menschheit.

The *Heilige Geschichte*'s importance is due not to the influence
that it exerted on Hess's contemporaries, for the book was completely disregarded, but rather to its being the first expression of
socialist thought in Germany, written a year before Weitling's
first book. The central theme of the *Heilige Geschichte* is how
mankind can regain union with God now that the original harmony has been lost. The history is 'sacred' because in it the life
of God is expressed. Hess's communist conception of the future
is one deduced from the past and so the book is divided into two
parts: 'The past, as the foundation of that which is to come' and
'the future as a consequence of that which has happened'. The
first part has three sections: the first, before Christ, was the
childhood of humanity, unconscious union with God when
harmony reigned founded on community of possessions. This
harmony became disjointed after Christ and the disharmony
reached a culmination in the Middle Ages which precipitated the
appearance of private property and the right of inheritance. The
third period, which prepared the way for a return to the original
social unity, began with Spinoza, the man who first pointed out the
way for this return, and culminated in the French Revolution.
In the second part, Hess described how the future communist
society would, through freedom and equality, heal the breach
made among mankind. He thought that this might come about
peaceably, but feared it more likely that the growing gap between
rich and poor would bring about a social revolution.

This pathetic book, so awkwardly written, is significant mainly
for the use Hess made of his French sources. The influence of
radicals like Leroux and Caset seems quite strong, though he may
also have taken a lot from German romantics like Franz v. Baader.
His criticism of heredity and his idea of a new supra-confessional
religion were both taken from the Saint-Simonians. Rousseau
seems to be the source of Hess's emphasis on natural equality and
Fourier is represented by his ideal of harmony, the 'jump' by
which it will be inaugurated, and his criticism of capitalism and
trade based on competition. Communism was for Hess the aim:

'community of goods' he described as the final goal of 'social life', and he was of the opinion that 'community of goods expresses the concept of equality at its clearest and sharpest',[1] since inequality was the root of all social evils. Because inequality was caused by property rights and inheritance, Hess repeatedly drew attention to the increasing distance between what he called respectively 'pauperism' and the 'aristocracy of wealth'. 'The physical need that is now beginning to dominate is caused by the growing wealth of one part of society and the growing poverty of the other. This disharmony, inequality, egoism will become much greater. It will reach a height that will terrify even the most stupid and hard-boiled. . .'.[2] However, in the hand of Providence, trade and industry were only means toward a final harmony. 'They drive the opposition of wealth and poverty to its climax, after reaching which, it must of necessity level itself out'.[3] The middle classes were fast disappearing and only laws stringently regulating trade and industry would be of any use.

Hess's pleading, prophecies and warnings found no response, and it is very doubtful whether Marx ever read the book. But if he had, he would have found there the first sketch of the theory of concentration of capital, pauperisation and revolution, theories to which he later tried to give a more scientific basis.

2. THE 'EUROPÄISCHE TRIARCHIE'

Hess's next book, *Die europäische Triarchie*, written while he was still at Cologne and the work that brought him to the attention of his contemporaries, had its origin in the quarrel between the Prussian Government and the Archbishop of Cologne on the question of mixed marriages. In the face of this controversy Hess decided to write a work on the Church and the state: this he incorporated in 1840 into a work with the title *Die europäische Triarchie*, so called in contrast to a work that had recently appeared with the title *Die europäische Pentarchie*, which advocated an alliance of Russia, Austria, Prussia, France and England. Hess argued for an exclusive alliance of Prussia with the two progressive powers of England and France.

The *Europäische Triarchie* marked a considerable advance on

[1] M. Hess, p. 51.   [2] Ibid. p. 62.   [3] Ibid. p. 64.

the *Heilige Geschichte*, where man appeared very much as a blind instrument of the world spirit. Here man was given back his autonomy by the concept of action which appeared here for the first time and was to be the central theme of Hess's writings from this time on.

The long introduction to the book dealt with Hegel and his disciples. Hess agreed that Hegel's system represented the ultimate in philosophy: he considered it 'the absolutely highest point of the philosophy of spirit'.[1] Yet he criticised Hegel on two grounds. Firstly, his system did not know its own limits: Hegel was in error when he thought that his philosophy was more than a philosophy of spirit and one that *eo ipso* also included action. For life was larger than philosophy. Secondly, Hegel's philosophy was one of the present and the past and failed to take in the future. His philosophy of history, said Hess, was more history than philosophy. A philosophy of history which, as did Hegel's, only tried to understand the past and the present as reasonable, had only half understood its task. Hess also took issue at the same time with the Young Hegelians whose negative rationalism prevented them from making any useful advance on Hegel. For both these criticisms of Hegel Hess specifically acknowledged his debt to A. v. Cieszkowski, whose *Prolegomena* was published in 1838 and who was the first to advocate a philosophy of action to enlarge Hegel's philosophy of spirit.

Nevertheless, Hess recognised the unique achievement of German philosophy, which 'has fulfilled its vocation and led us to complete truth'. But the corollary was: 'Now we must build bridges to take us back from heaven to earth'.[2] Hess advocated for this purpose a synthesis between the spiritual resources of Germany and the practical experience of France. The reformation had freed the state from the Church and given the world spiritual freedom. This work had been continued by German philosophy and particularly Hegel. But mere intellectual activity was not sufficient. The passage from ideas to action had been achieved by France, where the Revolution had continued the work of the Reformation in giving liberty a real expression. Thus 'from two sides, Germany and France, by the Reformation and the Revolution, a powerful impetus has already been given. The

[1] Ibid. p. 79.   [2] Ibid. p. 77.

only remaining task is to unite these two tendencies and to finish the work. England seems destined to achieve this and so our century ought to look above all in that direction'.[1]

The most important part of the *Europäische Triarchie* was the fifth chapter entitled 'Our Future, or Social and Political Freedom'. Here Hess proposed various ideas that were to have a great influence on his contemporaries. Since he was very conscious of the threat of censorship his language is sometimes very allusive. He certainly thought that the abolition of private property was essential to any new social order. A unified society was impossible if the entities comprising it had different interests. 'It follows that there must be no separation of ownership between individuals, families, etc., and so we must associate ourselves in order to realise the perfect condition of human society'.[2]

Hess was not at all clear as to how this future society would be realised. His general position seems to be that 'only the spiritual is the cause of social and moral loss of freedom' and thus that spiritual emancipation is a necessary preliminary of any other sort of emancipation. On the other hand, there is an interesting passage on the connexion between the means of production and men's social life, that Hess does not attempt to generalise, where with reference to Aristotle's definition of slaves as living tools he says that the more imperfect the inanimate tools the more men must be degraded to living tools. But with the progress of modern machinery this exploitation was no longer necessary and the freeing of the servile classes had become a possibility. There are, however, other passages in which Hess implies that social emancipation is very dependent on material factors of this kind. For instance, in the introduction he says:

> The opposition between poverty and the aristocracy of wealth is not only still with us and unconquered, it has not yet reached the level of revolution although it is already evident enough. But how can there be talk of an objective reconciliation in a world where we still see on the one side growing riches and on the other misery destroying itself in its own blood and sweat?'[3]

Later Hess says that this opposition certainly exists in Germany but that 'it is not nor will it become so marked as to bring about

[1] Ibid. p 105.   [2] Ibid. p. 153.   [3] Ibid. p. 96.

a revolutionary outbreak. The opposition of poverty and wealth will only reach the level of revolution in England. . .'.[1] Hess also lays strong emphasis on the role of the state and the necessity of a strong central government, which, in opposition to the liberals, he considered necessary for any real freedom: 'Order and freedom are not so opposed to each other that the one, carried to its highest degree, excludes the other. Rather the highest freedom is only conceivable in the highest order'.[2]

Unlike the *Heilige Geschichte*, the *Europäische Triarchie* was widely read and, his anonymity soon being broken, made Hess well known. Its influence on the Young Hegelians, Marx included, was profound. Its main achievement was to bring knowledge of communism into intellectual circles and to be the first manifestation of socialism after the somewhat general notions of Cieszkowski, following up his idea of a philosophy that could include the future and thus lead to action. It was this link of the philosophy at the time being elaborated by the Young Hegelians with the socialist doctrines of France that pointed the way forward along the path that Marx was to take. Hess's book placed social questions clearly in the forefront and his French parallels were not, like Heine's, political, but social: he likened Hegel to Saint-Simon and Fichte to Proudhon. As Hess himself wrote later, the chief service of the book was 'that it presented to the public, in a veiled and mystic fashion, an idea that could not yet be expressed in a clear and precise manner . . . the idea of socialism'.[3] Nevertheless, the idea was still 'veiled and mysterious' and the immediate effect of the book was more through its advocacy of a philosophy of action and in particular its parallels between Germany and France and the necessity of Germany's seeking a complement to her philosophy from the other side of the Rhine. This was taken up by all the Young Hegelians and by Marx in particular in his 'zur Einleitung Kritik der Hegelschen Rechtsphilosophie'. The idea, too, quoted above, of the influence of economic factors on social evolution was also taken up by Marx, for what Hess is in fact saying with his different levels of the gap between poverty and wealth is that the true freedom of all men can only be attained when the opposition between capitalism and labour has been done away with by revolution. Hess's view of the

[1] Ibid. p. 107.   [2] Ibid. p. 156.   [3] Ibid. p. 301.

unity of spirit and nature, that is of ideas and matter, is also a forerunner of Marx's. It is this view that leads Hess to say now that the spiritual is the primary sphere on which all else depends and now to talk of the economic conditions necessary for any successful change of the social order. This same desire for unity caused Marx to emphasise the material side, and the same resultant contradictions appear in Marx's later writings and particularly the Paris MSS., for instance: 'We see how consistent naturalism and humanism are distinguished both from idealism and materialism and at the same time constitute their unifying truth'.[1] The ambiguities contained in this doctrine, particularly when it comes to formulating a programme for action, are clearly shown by the subsequent difficulties and divisions of Marx's followers.

3. HESS AND THE 'RHEINISCHE ZEITUNG'

After the publication of the *Europäische Triarchie* Hess still worked in his father's factory in Cologne and planned to write a larger work on the philosophy of action. However, the founding of the *Rheinische Zeitung* gave him his longed-for chance of independence. The *Rheinische Zeitung* was financed by liberal Rhenish industrialists who wished to have a paper strongly supporting free enterprise in the face of the Catholic and conservative *Kölnische Zeitung*, the dominant paper in the Rhineland up to that time. Hess played a large part in the negotiations and canvassing for support that went on before the paper started publication – one of those concerned called him 'the spirit of the whole enterprise'. But much to his dismay he was only given the post of sub-editor. No doubt the men behind the paper were afraid of his well-known socialist tendencies. As it was, Hess was still able to carry on his missionary activities since his special charge on the paper was anything dealing with France which was then, and for some time to come, the homeland of socialist ideas.

Hess's articles in the *Rheinische Zeitung* followed up the themes of the *Europäische Triarchie*. The most remarkable was on

[1] K. Marx, *Frühe Schriften* I, p. 650.

England and the imminence of a catastrophe there. The emphasis with which Hess described the widening gap between the classes
and the utter inadequacy of any merely political reforms that left
untouched the social evils deserves a lengthy quotation:

> All political reforms would merely be a palliative for an evil
> which in the final analysis is not political but social. No form
> of government has created this evil, none will heal it. When in
> the face of the bad social conditions that are about to attain
> their climax in England people say that always, in all states,
> under all governments, there have been rich and poor, I can
> only say that this, far from being a consolation, shows that not
> even the most radical political reform is capable of changing
> these conditions. The objective causes that will provoke a
> catastrophe in England are not of a political character. In-
> dustry passing from the hands of the people into those of the
> capitalists, the trade that used to be carried out on a small
> scale by small traders more and more being controlled by large-
> scale capitalists, adventurers and swindlers, land property
> concentrated by the laws of heredity in the hands of aristocratic
> usurers . . . all these conditions that exist everywhere, but
> principally in England and which constitute, if not the exclu-
> sive, at least the principal and essential causes of the catastrophe
> that threatens us, have a social and not a political character.[1]

The other articles in the *Rheinische Zeitung* followed the same
line: one on the political parties in Germany interpreted the
French Revolution as the seizing of power by the middle classes, a
process that ended in the July Revolution and emphasised that
the nineteenth century had problems that required a totally
different solution. Of course, since these articles were written for
a paper that was supposed to be the *porte parole* of the Rhenish
trading bourgeoisie, Hess had to be careful how he chose his
words: it was usually safer to put over his ideas at second hand.
He gave the book of Lorenz v. Stein *Sozialismus und Kommunismus
des heutigen Frankreichs* a laudatory review, detailed in another
article Wilhelm Weitling's ideas on the organisation of a future
communist society and even published a manifesto issued by the
French communists. These articles do indeed show a certain

[1] M. Hess, op. cit. p. 184.

amount of the influence of Feuerbach: here, for the first time, Hess uses the typically Feuerbachian term 'species' (*Gattung*) and he mentions Feuerbach in the letter to Auerbach quoted below. But this influence is very far from being as exclusive as some believe. Hess borrows as much, if not more, from Bruno Bauer as he does from Feuerbach. For example, progress in the workshops of industry and progress in the workshops of the spirit are said to be 'children of one and the same father – free self-consciousness'.[1] Also his view of the importance of pure negation – 'negation is the essential thing; we must destroy in order to put things in motion; it is by virtue of this that the negative includes the positive'[2] – is very much in the spirit of Bruno Bauer. Hess is, as usual, extremely eclectic and with difficulty classifiable as the disciple of anyone in particular.

It was during this period that Hess met Karl Marx for the first time. Marx had come to Bonn in April 1841 to collaborate with Bruno Bauer and in the hope of getting a post at the university there. Hess was extremely impressed by his first meeting with Marx, as his subsequent letter to Auerbach shows: 'Dr. Marx . . . will give mediaeval religion and politics their *coup de grâce*. He combines the deepest philosophical seriousness with the most biting wit. Imagine Rousseau, Voltaire, Holbach, Lessing, Heine and Hegel fused into one person, fused, I say, not thrown together in a heap, and you have Dr. Marx'.[3] Marx, however, was at this time very suspicious of socialist and communist doctrines and Hess had at first very little success in his direction. Indeed, in the one piece of writing where Marx alludes to Hess he seems completely to have missed the point. For he criticised an article by Hess on 'The Question of Centralisation in France and Germany' as being too abstract and utopian: 'Philosophy can only protest energetically when it is mistaken for imagination. The fiction of a "righteous" people is as much a stranger to philosophy as the fiction of a "pious hyena" can be to nature. The author substitutes his own abstractions for philosophy'.[4] This criticism, however, betrays a complete misunderstanding of Hess.

[1] M. Hess, op. cit. p. 153.
[2] Cf. J. Hansen, *Gustav v. Mevissen* (Berlin, 1906) I, p. 93.
[3] M. Hess, *Briefwechsel*, p. 80.
[4] *MEGA*, I, i. 1, p. 231.

So far from being 'abstract', he follows up his statement that the division between individual and collective would be no problem if all were righteous by saying: 'But the point here is not to answer the question of centralisation in a theoretical, philosophical, abstract manner, but in an empirical and relative fashion; the question is what is preferable *under the prevailing circumstances...*',[1] Hess then goes on to give a very concrete historical analysis of the different solutions to the problem in France and Germany. Nevertheless, Marx cannot have failed to be in some way marked by Hess's propaganda in favour of communist ideas and it is no doubt largely owing to this propaganda that communism should become suddenly so spoken about in the years 1842–3.

When in October 1842 Marx moved from Bonn to Cologne, his contact with Hess was closer and he participated in the regular discussions of a club of socialists whose chairman was Hess and whose members included Mevissen and Jung who had helped finance the *Rheinische Zeitung* and Karl d'Ester who later had a leading role in the communist movement. When the *Augsburger Allgemeine Zeitung* attacked the *Rheinische Zeitung* as being a vehicle of communist propaganda because of its publication of Hess's articles, the duty of replying to this attack fell to Marx in his first article written as editor. He repudiated the charge violently: 'The *Rheinische Zeitung* which does not even concede a theoretical reality to communist ideas and which hopes even less for their practical realisation, which it does not anyway consider possible, proposes to submit these ideas to a serious critical analysis'. Marx does, however, refer to the 'penetrating' book of Proudhon, admits that communist ideas cannot be refuted by superficial judgements and ends with words full of omen for the future: communist action can always be suppressed by force, but 'ideas which gain a hold on our intelligence, our soul, our conscience, are chains from which we cannot tear ourselves loose without tearing our hearts, devils that we can only conquer by submission to them'.[2]

Hess had a much better effect on Engels whom he converted completely to the communist cause. Engels had finished his military service and left Berlin *en route* for England to work in one of his father's factories in Manchester. He stopped in Cologne

<hr>

[1] M. Hess, p. 176.   [2] Marx–Engels, *Werke*, I, p. 108.

to see the editors of the *Rheinische Zeitung* for which he wanted
to do some writing. Although he was coldly received by Marx,
who saw in him a representative of the Berlin *Freien*, he had
a long session with Hess who later described it to his friend
Auerbach as follows: 'We talked about questions of the day and
he, an out-and-out revolutionary, parted from me the keenest of
communists'.[1] Hess kept in close touch with Engels while he
was in England and his association was much closer with him than
with Marx. They worked together during 1845–6, organising
the communist meetings at Elberfeld, and Engels was co-editor
of Hess's newspaper *Gesellschaftsspiegel*. Engels had a great
admiration for Hess whom he described in the following year as
'the first communist in the party'[2] and the 'first to reach communism by the philosophical path'.

4. ESSAYS IN '21 BOGEN AUS DER SCHWEIZ'

It was while he was still in Paris as a correspondent of the
Rheinische Zeitung that Hess wrote the articles later published in
21 Bogen aus der Schweiz, a collection of articles by various hands
that had been refused by the German censorship. Hess's articles
here were called by Marx, together with the works of Weitling
and Engels, 'the only substantial and original works written in
German in this field' (i.e. political economy).

The first of these articles, entitled 'Sozialismus und Kommunismus', was an extended review of a book by Lorenz v. Stein,
Sozialismus und Kommunismus des heutigen Frankreichs. Stein
was described by Hess as a middle-of-the-road Hegelian; he had
been sent by the Prussian government to Paris to report on the
socialist movement and this book was the result. Hess started his
criticism by giving his opinion of the present situation of France
and Germany. No nation was as unpractical as Germany whose
theoretical achievements – the best of any nation – were in sharp
contrast with the realities of her situation. But it was nevertheless only from Germany that a philosophy of action could come,

---

[1] M. Hess, *Briefwechsel*, p. 103.

[2] Marx–Engels, *Werke*, I, p. 494.

for only in Germany had philosophy reached its culminating point. France, by contrast, was too one-sidedly practical: the Revolution there had tried to reform politics as Kant had tried to reform religion by making it 'rational'. But for politics as for religion, abolition was necessary not reform. The two men who were at the origin of this process were Fichte and Babeuf: 'Atheism in Germany dates from Fichte and from Babeuf in France dates communism, or, as Proudhon now more accurately expresses it, anarchy, that is the negation of all political domination, the negation of the concepts of the state and politics'.[1]

This parallelism between French political events and German philosophy had been started by Heine in his book *Zur Geschichte der Philosophie und Religion in Deutschland* (1835). Hess, however, changes the parallel in a way very indicative of his different point of view. Only 'the phantasy of a poet',[2] he says, could think French 'politics' parallel with German philosophy; rather was Schelling analogous to Saint-Simon and Hegel to Fourier. It was thanks to these men that progress had been made beyond Fichte and Babeuf. Fourier had solved the problem of equality and Hegel had solved the problem of freedom and Proudhon had brought in the question of property. Now the absolute equality of France and the absolute freedom in Germany must unite. Without the absolute equality of French communism on the one hand and without the absolute freedom of German atheism on the other, personal freedom and social equality could not become a reality.

> As long as a condition of contradiction and dependence finds recognition in the objective world, as long as *politics* rules the world, then the liberation of this world from the fetters of heavenly politics is also inconceivable. Religion and politics stand and fall with each other.[3]

In his book Stein had rightly laid emphasis on equality as a central principle of French communism. But he only saw its negative side: an attempt by the workers to obtain enjoyment of goods equal to that of the possessing class. But this was a misconception, for 'it is precisely one of the leading characteristics of communism that in it the opposition of enjoyment and labour

[1] M. Hess, *Aufsätze*, p. 199.   [2] Ibid. p. 200.   [3] Ibid. p. 202.

disappears'.[1] It was only recently that the principles of equality
and freedom and the means of achieving them had been understood in all their depth.

> Work, and society in general, is not to be organised, it will
> organise itself of its own accord in that each person does what
> he cannot leave undone and leaves alone what he cannot do.
> Every man has an inclination to some kind of activity, even to
> very different sorts of activity and out of the multiplicity of
> free human inclinations and activities arises the free, living and
> ever-youthful organism of free, human society, free, human
> occupations that cease to be 'work' and become identical with
> 'pleasure'.[2]

Stein, however, was only a 'middle-of-the-road Hegelian' and
as such could not be expected to understand the positive aspect
of current affairs. He did not concentrate enough on the development of communist ideas, but just catalogued them. He emphasised the connexion between communism and the proletariat but
did not deal sufficiently with the justification of the communists'
demands.

The second of these articles, entitled 'Philosophie der Tat', was
an attempt to give communism a philosophical basis. Fichte's
concept of the activity of the self was central to Hess's thesis.
What I know, according to Hess, is that I think that I am
intellectually active. This intellectual activity is the source of all
reality. 'If this act is only half completed and what thinks kept
different from what is thought, then spirit is banging its head
against a wall, against a barrier that it has itself created and not
broken through. It wanders into a cul-de-sac and action is
blocked'.[3] Self-consciousness is turned into a theological consciousness. 'When what thinks and what is thought are separate, real life and the living self appear as outside both. . . . This
externally imagined life is an empty reflexion of the empty self,
the shadow of a shadow, the theological God. . .'.[4] Thus all
ideas and objects were in the final analysis to be recognised by
self-consciousness as belonging to itself. Hence the necessity of
atheism.

[1] Ibid. p. 207.   [2] Ibid. pp. 207f.
[3] M. Hess, *Aufsätze*, p. 210.   [4] Ibid. p. 210.

Hess then moved from philosophy to politics and religion, for 'social freedom is either the result of intellectual freedom or it is baseless. . .'.[1] He once again pointed out that German philosophy was as ignorant of socialism as French socialists were of German thinking on religion. The essence of both religion and politics was that they allowed the real life of real individuals to be absorbed by an abstract, unreal universal. The revolutions of the past had not really achieved anything. 'The revolution has left the dualism intact . . . the spiritual as well as the social revolution, the German as well as the French, has really left everything as it was'.[2] Even the Young Hegelians were still stuck fast in a theological consciousness, they still opposed the individual to the state and, at most, attained to a liberal anarchy from which they relapsed into some conception of the theological state. The true goal was activity that was voluntary. The essential thing about atheism, communism and anarchy was that people should limit themselves and not be limited by anything in which they did not acquiesce. To establish this a revolution would be necessary, nor would it be long delayed since, after the bad times of the Restoration, the forces of atheism and communism were now on the increase.

The third and much smaller article, entitled 'Die eine und ganze Freiheit' merely repeated that it would be no use trying to achieve intellectual freedom without social freedom and vice versa, and emphasised that the 'life-blood' of this freedom was the unity of work and pleasure.

It has been said that in these articles the influence of Feuerbach is predominant. But it is not until the end of 1843 and the publication of the *Deutsch-französische Jahrbücher* that Hess is fully a disciple of Feuerbach. He uses Feuerbach's favourite term 'species' once but otherwise there is nothing to show Feuerbach's influence. To say, as does H. Arvon,[3] that the articles of Hess constantly refer to the fundamental themes of the 'Grundsätze' of Feuerbach, as though there were some question of influence, is simply incorrect, as the 'Grundsätze' were published some months *after* Hess wrote his articles. The vocabulary and content, particularly of the second article, 'Philosophie der Tat',

---

[1] Ibid. p. 214.   [2] Ibid. p. 217.

[3] H. Arvon, *Ludvig Feuerbach* (Paris 1957) p. 107.

are much more in the style of Bruno Bauer. Hess was certainly familiar with Bauer's ideas at this time: his were some of the few lectures that Hess, in company with Marx, attended in 1841–2 and he certainly read his publications, for he refers to the *Posaune* twice in these articles. When Hess talked about the unity of German philosophy and French socialism, the philosophy he meant was that of the Young Hegelians who were to him the representatives of the 'newest philosophy'. Bauer was recognised at this time (immediately after his dismissal) as the leading Young Hegelian. According to his convert, Engels, Hess considered communism as the necessary consequence of the Young Hegelian philosophy.

A careful reading particularly of the 'Philosophie der Tat' will show that the influence of Bauer is very strong. The idea that the self-conscious ego was fundamental, that this self-conscious-ness has stages, and that the whole of previous history is nothing but the development of spirit, which, in order to become real, has had to become opposed to itself, was completely in the spirit of Bauer. From Bauer, too, came the idea of a two-term dialectic and the rejection of all mediation: 'There can no longer be any talk of a "compromise" between communism and the principle of private property. From now on begins the genuine and conscious struggle of principles'.

These articles undoubtedly exercised a considerable influence on Marx. What they did was to demonstrate that the state and private property were also forms of the self-alienation of man and that therefore criticism must become political and social as well as philosophical and religious. Hess was the first to make the all-important link between philosophy and French communism, as Marx himself said in the introduction to the Paris MSS. quoted above and Engels, too, in one of his articles for the *New Moral World*. What Hess did was to introduce the idea of development into Feuerbach's static concept of man and thus give his anthro-pology a historical dimension and also to point the way to a possible positive outcome of the negative criticism of the Young Hegelians. Marx was enabled by personal contact with Hess and a study of his writings to go beyond the vaguely liberal, demo-cratic position that he held at the end of 1842. The 'Einleitung zur Kritik der Hegelschen Rechtsphilosophie', written at the end

of 1843, already shows the influence of Hess: the basic thesis that
Germany, because of her predominant philosophical position, can
produce a revolution that will bring her to the forefront of European progress is one already put forward by Hess in the opening of
'Sozialismus und Kommunismus' and the picture of the proletariat here as the emancipator of the whole of society is very
near that of Hess who never really accepted the idea of the class
struggle. But it is even more in certain passages of the Paris
MSS., Marx's first piece of writing after his conversion to communism, that the influence of Hess is apparent. Marx himself
acknowledges his debt to Hess in his criticism of private property:

> Private property has made us so stupid and partial that an
> object is only *ours* when we have it, when it exists for us as
> capital or when it is directly eaten, drunk, worn, inhabited, etc.,
> in short utilised in some way.... Thus all the physical and
> intellectual senses have been replaced by the simple alienation
> of *all* these senses: the sense of *having* (on the category of
> *having* see Hess in *21 Bogen*).[1]

It is in what may be called the 'eschatological' passages of the
Paris MSS. that Marx is most clearly at one with the spirit of
Hess. The prophecy of the final and definitive setting aside of all
barriers, the gaining of ultimate unity here on this earth, this
yearning that is to be found in all of Hess's writings is well
expressed in a famous passage of the Paris MSS.:

> Communism is the true solution of the conflict between exist-
> ence and essence, between objectification and self-affirmation,
> between freedom and necessity, between the individual and
> species. It is the solution of the riddle of history and knows
> itself to be this solution.[2]

5. HESS AND THE 'DEUTSCH-FRANZÖSISCHE JAHRBÜCHER

Hess occupied the months after the essays in *21 Bogen* with
miscellaneous writing – an appreciation of Wilhelm Weitling,

[1] K. Marx, *Frühe Schriften*, I, p. 599.   [2] Ibid. p. 594.

favourable on the whole, but criticising him for not being philosophical enough, and a manifesto entitled 'What we Want', that
remained unpublished. This contained much the same ideas as
the 'Philosophie der Tat', but reversed Hess's former ideas on
the question of centralisation, as here he favours the erection of
the smallest possible social entities.

After the suppression of the *Rheinische Zeitung*, Hess returned
to Cologne and remained there until August continuing his
proselytising of which he gives this account to Auerbach:

> Since the *Rheinische Zeitung* ceased publication, while I was
> still in Paris, I devoted myself exclusively to the philosophical
> development of communism . . . and have the joy to see that
> my activity is not fruitless. The Young Hegelians are already
> in part won over. . . . I can tell you this much, that I am
> beginning to put my theory of the Triarchy into practice; I
> have connections for this end in Germany, France and England.[1]

So when Ruge, together with Marx and Fröbel, set about trying
to create a replacement for the *Rheinische Zeitung*, Hess naturally
joined them. Ruge visited him in Cologne and the two set off to
Brussels to see whether it would be a suitable place from which to
edit the new journal. They thought not, and moved on to Paris
where Hess introduced Ruge to the communists whose acquaint-
ance he had made during his previous stay – Dezamy, Blanc and
Leroux. Marx arrived soon after and he and Hess were in close
contact as forming part of the circle centred on the *Deutsch-
französische Jahrbücher*, which included Heine and Herwegh.
The reputation that Hess enjoyed at this time is difficult to judge:
Ruge talks of him rather patronisingly and his later views are
distorted by his quarrel with Hess, but Heine at least speaks of
Hess as 'one of the most outstanding of our political writers'.[2]
Hess occupied his time in Paris by writing articles for German
newspapers and also in writing an essay intended for the *Deutsch-
französische Jahrbücher*, which was, from the point of view of his
influence on Marx, his most important piece of work – the essay
'On the Essence of Money'.

[1] M. Hess, *Briefwechsel*, p. 103.
[2] *H. Heines Briefwechsel*, ed. F. Hirth (Munich and Berlin, 1917) II,
p. 469.

This essay was written at the end of 1843 or the beginning of 1844 and intended for the *Deutsch-französische Jahrbücher*. Hess had already delivered most of the article to the editors when it was decided, owing to financial difficulties, that the first number of the *Deutsch-französische Jahrbücher* would also be the last, and so Hess's article was not published. As Hess wrote two years later in a polemic directed against Ruge:

> When the *Deutsch-französische Jahrbücher* were founded in Paris, I obtained from Fröbel and Graziano,[1] the backers of the journal, an advance for work that I had already delivered to them and also for some that was destined for the journal and was still in my hands although almost completed (among these latter there was an essay 'Über das Geldwesen' of which I had already delivered the larger part to the editors of the *Deutsch-französische Jahrbücher* and which appeared only one and a half years later simply because Graziano's *Jahrbücher* ceased publication soon after their beginning. . .).[2]

Thus Marx must have read at least most of Hess's article before writing his own, all the more so because Ruge was ill at the time and so all the editorial responsibility fell on Marx. Hess certainly had the impression that his article had been a seminal one, for he wrote of it:

> The best recent writings on the essence of money have adopted ideas that I developed, that is, that money is for the practical world what God is for the theoretical world, that it constitutes the alienation of the idea of social value, in silver or alloy from the Catholic point of view, or in paper money from the Protestant point of view. In other words, money is simply the inorganic symbol of our present social production that has broken free from our rational control and therefore dominates us.[3]

Whether Hess had Marx specifically in mind or not when he wrote this, the similarities between Hess's article and Marx's 'Judenfrage' are remarkable and can only be accounted for on the sup-

[1] Hess's nickname for Ruge.

[2] M. Hess, 'Dottore Graziano oder Doktor Arnold Ruge in Paris', in *Die Gesellschaft* (1931) I, 178 f.   [3] Ibid.

position that Marx copied heavily from Hess's essay presuming it would not be published.

The importance of Hess's essay is that it is the first attempt to employ Feuerbach's idea of religious alienation to the fields of economic and social life. This idea had already been extended, in the atmosphere of rapid secularisation current among the Young Hegelians, to the field of political life. Hess was the first to go deeper to the more fundamental, as he thought, level of economics. To see this progression, we have only to compare the definition of life as 'activity' at the beginning of Hess's essay 'Philosophie der Tat', written a year earlier,[1] with that at the beginning of the 'Über das Geldwesen': 'Life is the exchange of productive activity'.[2] The theme of Hess's article is that the co-operation between men involved in this exchanging has evolved to such a point that it is now capable of being perfected. But in present society man is separated from his social essence theoretically through religion and practically through the power of money that has enslaved all men. All values are expressed in terms of money and the result is a slavery worse than that of antiquity. Society is atomised since the medieval corporations have been dissolved by such anti-social conceptions as that of the Rights of Man. This is aided by the religious alienation present in Christianity, but Judaism represents in their grossest form the evils of bourgeois society, the symbol of which is money. This form of society has now outlived itself and must yield to one based on love.

In Marx's articles there is the same view of the Rights of Man as the typical expression of contemporary bourgeois society and as a regress on the corporations and closely knit communities of the Middle Ages. Hess says:

Practical egoism was sanctioned in that men were declared to be single individuals, and true men to be abstract, naked persons; the Rights of Man were proclaimed as the rights of independent men, and so as the independence of men from each other. Their separation and individualisation was said to be the essence of life and freedom and isolated persons were branded as free, true and natural men.[3]

[1] M. Hess, *Aufsätze*, p. 210.
[2] Ibid. p. 330.   [3] Ibid. p. 339.

And again:

> We are complete and conscious egoists who sanction in free competition the war of all against all and in the so-called Rights of Man the rights of isolated individuals, private people. . . .[1]

Marx, in his 'Zur Judenfrage', deals with the rights one by one and echoes this criticism. He says for example:

> The right to freedom is based not on the linking of men to each other but rather on the separation of man from man. It is the right to this separation, the right of an individual limited to himself.[2] As for the right to property, the effect of this is that each man sees in the other not the realisation but rather the limitation of his own freedom.[3]

Hess thinks that the situation in the Middle Ages was by no means so bad: the possessions of some men at least had a social significance and character. The estates and corporations were indeed egoistic associations, but they had a social character and a communal spirit, though it was a limited one: 'the individual could become part of his social sphere of work and fuse, in an incomplete way, with the community'.[4] Marx's view of the estates and corporations is very similar; feudal society had, according to him, an immediately political character, that is, 'the elements of civic life, like property, family, method of work were raised to elements in the state's life in the form of sovereignty, estate and corporations'[5] and *pro tanto* united men instead of splitting them up.

Hess and Marx are equally in agreement that it is the 'social' element in all questions that is the most important. For Hess the real essence of individuals, their real power is in the exchange of their products, commerce and co-operation. All thought and activity has its origin in the trade and working together of men.[6] For Marx the solution to the Jewish question is on similar lines: 'The question of Jewish emancipation changes itself for us into the question of what particular 'social' element is to be overcome

[1] Ibid. p. 345. [2] K. Marx, *Frühe Schriften*, I, p. 473.
[3] Ibid. [4] M. Hess, op. cit. p. 343.
[5] K. Marx, *Frühe Schriften*, I, p. 476.
[6] M. Hess, *Aufsätze*, p. 331.

in order to emancipate the Jews?'[1] The answer to this question is identical for Hess and Marx: it is the same sort of alienation as obtains in the religious sphere that now exists in the economic sphere, too, and is symbolised by money. 'What God is for the theoretical life', said Hess, 'money is for the practical life of the inverted world: the alienated power of men, their reified activity'.[2] This money, according to both Hess and Marx, had reduced everything, even down to love itself, to dependence on it. 'Money', said Hess, 'is the worth of men expressed in figures, the hallmark of our slavery'.[3] The modern world is one where 'nothing, from the most natural form of love to the exchange of ideas in the educated world, can be effected without money'.[4] And Marx:

> Money is the jealous God of Israel beside which no other God may exist. Money abases all the gods of mankind and changes them into commodities. Money is the universal and self sufficient value of all things ... even the species-relation itself, the relation between man and woman, becomes an object of commerce.[5]

This state of affairs, according to Hess, has one of its greatest supports in the Christian religion: 'Christianity is the theory, the logic of egoism'.[6] 'The essence of the modern world, money, is the realised essence of Christianity'.[7] The climax has been achieved in the Jews whose vocation it is to develop the predatory animal in mankind and who have fulfilled this vocation.[8] Marx is of the same opinion:

> From the beginning, the Christian was the theorising Jew; consequently, the Jew is the practical Christian. And the practical Christian has become a Jew again. ... Christianity is the sublime thought of Judaism; Judaism is the vulgar, practical application of Christianity. But this practical application could only become universal when Christianity as a perfected religion had accomplished, in a theoretical fashion, the alienation of man from himself and from nature.[9]

---

[1] K. Marx, op. cit. p. 481.   [2] M. Hess, *Aufsätze*, pp. 334f.

[3] Ibid. p. 335.   [4] Ibid. p. 339.

[5] K. Marx, *Frühe Schriften*, I, p. 484.   [6] M. Hess, op. cit. p. 334.

[7] M. Hess, op. cit. p. 337.   [8] Cf. M. Hess, *Aufsätze*, p. 345.

[9] K. Marx, *Frühe Schriften*, I, p. 486.

These parallels between the two texts are more than enough to justify the statement that Marx copied Hess's ideas at this stage. Certainly it is from Hess that he borrows all his leading themes at this turning point in his development when he begins to make the economic sphere the object of his immediate attention. Hess's article also contains certain doctrines that Marx only enunciated later, for instance that the principal evil of capitalist society resides in over-production and this causes the search for wider markets.[1]

The ideas in the Paris MSS. on alienation as englobing both the worker and the capitalist are twice emphasised here by Hess.[2] The opening section 'Über das Geldwesen'[3] about the origin and development of man's trade and commerce viewed in its natural and social framework recalls the famous first statement of historical materialism at the beginning of the *Deutsche Ideologie*, and Hess's next section on the theme that 'thought and activity have their sole basis in the trade and co-operation of individuals'[4] points forward to Marx's doctrine of the relation of basis and superstructure and his concept of ideology.

Thus at the beginning of 1844 it was Hess who was setting the pace, but his article, once read by Marx, lay idle in a drawer for one and a half years before being published in an obscure journal and forgotten. It has been called 'one of the most important publications of early German socialist literature',[5] but it took a louder and more persistent voice to convey its message.

6. Hess from 1844 to 1848

From the demise of the *Deutsch-französische Jahrbücher* until this final break between Hess and Marx in February 1848 it is extremely difficult to characterise the writings of Hess which are even more inconsistent than usual. This is due to the fact that

[1] Cf. M. Hess, op. cit. p. 333.
[2] Cf. M. Hess, op. cit. pp. 335, 341 f.
[3] Cf. M. Hess, op. cit. p. 330.
[4] M. Hess, op. cit. p. 331.
[5] E. Silberner, 'Die Tätigkeit von Moses Hess', *Annali*, p. 431.

Hess, particularly in 1846–7, was trying his best to make his own certain aspects of the system that Marx was evolving – aspects that were incompatible with Hess's fundamental outlook. The result is that though there are many passages in his writings of this time that look very 'marxist', yet he always reverts to that form of socialism which he originated and is generally known as 'true socialism'. This type of socialism drew its inspiration from the philosophy of Feuerbach and its principal exponent at this time together with Hess was Karl Grün an ardent disciple of Feuerbach who later edited his letters. Central to it was Feuerbach's concept of a human nature or 'species' and this socialism was 'true' in so far as it promoted the realisation of this species. The most important factor in this human essence was love, which was to be the foundation of the new society. Thus most of true socialist writing consists of an advocacy of love and preaching against the selfishness and egoism that prevent the realisation of this society. This excluded any appeal to force and any rigid doctrine of the class struggle. Socialism was justified by an appeal to moral ideals, because it was right and just, not because it was necessary and inevitable. The human essence to which Hess appealed was something common to all men and not radically impaired by their position in society.

At the beginning of 1844 Hess returned to Cologne to his father's home, resumed his studies and continued to write articles among which 'Die Sozialistische Bewegung in Deutschland' was the first attempt to write a history of German socialism. Hess at this time broke with Ruge who (according to Hess – unfortunately we have no account by Ruge of the affair) insistently demanded the repayment of the advance he had given Hess for articles in the *Deutsch-französische Jahrbücher*. The difference was also no doubt somewhat deeper than this as Ruge was opposed to communist ideas and broke soon afterwards with Marx. At the end of 1844 Hess published in *Vorwärts*, the communist paper in Paris, a catechism of communism entitled 'Kommunistisches Bekenntnis in Fragen und Antworten'. This document is the immediate predecessor of the *Communist Manifesto*, itself also drafted at first in the form of question and answer. It contains a section on religion typical of the true socialist view of which the first two questions are: 'What religion ought we all to confess? The religion of love and humanity. Where is the home of this religion? In the hearts of all good men'.[1] This sort of talk was totally unacceptable to Marx and the difference was later to become clear. Nearer to Marx was Hess's anticipation of the slogan later to become famous: 'Work according to capacity and consumption according to need is the true principle of a rational union'.

At the end of 1844 Hess wrote a small brochure entitled *Die letzten Philosophen*, which consisted principally of a criticism of Stirner (whose book had just appeared) with remarks also on Bruno Bauer and Feuerbach. Hess's main criticism of Stirner was, naturally, of his egoism that turned society into a war of all against all. Stirner wishes to return to the animal kingdom and Hess repeats the criticism of individualism and the Rights of Man that he had already used in 'Über das Geldwesen'. The remarks on Feuerbach are interesting, for though at the end of the article he says that if Stirner and Bauer were to learn from each other they would be able to imitate Feuerbach and develop towards socialism, yet at the beginning of the article his attitude towards Feuerbach is a critical one: Feuerbach 'admits that this essence (that is, of man) exists in each individual man who acknowledges it, which is a philosophical untruth and some idea of the modern state, since the species-being only realises itself in a society where all men can form themselves, fulfil themselves and develop their activities'.[2] This foreshadows in a very general way, as indeed does the criticism of Stirner, the later work of Marx in the *Deutsche Ideologie*. Thereafter Hess continued to collaborate desultorily with Marx and Engels and even contributed a chapter to the *Deutsche Ideologie*, but they soon drifted apart, though Hess continued to be a staunch supporter of Marx in the First International.

[1] M. Hess, *Aufsätze*, p. 366.   [2] Ibid. p. 384.

CONCLUSION

THE above attempts to show Marx's specific debts to his contemporaries are in no way intended to devalue the importance and even the originality of his doctrines. It is a truism that every person's ideas are the product of their age. And Marx, having an exceptionally perceptive mind, gained an immense amount from contact with his contemporaries. From Bauer he took his incisive, and even macabre, criticism of religion which served as a model for his analysis of politics, economics, etc.; from Feuerbach he took over a systematic transformation of Hegel's philosophy, rejecting the supremacy of the Hegelian Idea and starting from a radical humanism; Stirner, the most negative of all the Young Hegelians, compelled Marx to go beyond the somewhat static humanism of Feuerbach; finally, Hess, the first propagator of communist ideas in Germany, pioneered the application of radical ideas in the field of economics. The demonstration of these influences, and even borrowings, does not imply any diminution of Marx's intellectual stature. On the contrary: it is only a knowledge of the contemporary intellectual scene and of the concepts peculiar to it that enable a just appreciation of so complex a thinker.

SELECT BIBLIOGRAPHY

(A) HEGEL
TEXTS

Hegel, G. W. F. *Sämtliche Werke*, ed. H. Glockner and J. Hoffmeister, Leipzig, 1925 ff.

TRANSLATIONS

Hegel, G. W. F. *The Phenomenology of Mind*, trans. J. B. Baillie, London and New York, Allen & Unwin, 2 vols., 1910.
Hegel, G. W. F. *Hegel's Philosophy of Right*, trans. T. M. Knox, Oxford, 1942.
Hegel, G. W. F. *Hegel's Political Writings*, trans. Sir Malcolm Knox, with introduction by Z. A. Pelczynski, Oxford, 1964.
Hegel, G. W. F. *Phénoménologie de l'esprit*, trans. Hippolyte, Paris, 2 vols., 1939-4.

COMMENTARIES

Findlay, J. N. *Hegel: A Re-examination*, Allen & Unwin, London, 1958.
Hippolyte, J. *Genèse et structure de la phénoménologie de l'esprit de Hégel*, Paris, 1947.
Kaufmann, W. *Hegel*, New York, 1965.
Kojève, A. *Introduction à la lecture de Hégel*, Paris, 1947.
Niel, H. *De la médiation dans la philosophie de Hégel*, Paris, 1945.

(B) THE YOUNG HEGELIANS
TEXTS

Die Hegelsche Linke, ed. K. Löwith, Stuttgart, 1962.

COMMENTARIES

Droz, J., Ayçoberry, P. 'Structures sociales et courants idéologiques en Allemagne prérévolutionnaire', in *Annali*, vi, Milan, 1963, pp. 164–236.
Erdmann, J. *Grundriß der Geschichte der Philosophie*, vol. 2, 2nd ed., Berlin, 1870.
Gebhardt, J. *Politik und Eschatologie. Studien zur Geschichte der Hegelschen Schule in den Jahren 1830-1840*, Munich, 1963.
Groethuysen, B. 'Les Jeunes Hégéliens et les origines du socialisme contemporain en Allemagne', in *Revue de Philosophie*, vol. 95.

Hook, S. *From Hegel to Marx*, London, 1936, reissued 1962.

Koigen, D. *Zur Vorgeschichte des modernen philosophischen Socialismus in Deutschland*, Berne, 1901.

Lobkowicz, N. *Theory and Practice from Aristotle to Marx*, Notre Dame, 1967.

Löwith, K. *Von Hegel zu Nietzsche*, 2nd ed., Stuttgart, 1950.

Mayer, G. 'Die Anfänge des politischen Radikalismus im vormärzlichen Preußen,' in *Zeitschrift für Politik*, 1931, pp. 1–117.

Mayer, G. 'Die Junghegelianer und der Preußischer Staat', in *Historische Zeitschrift*, 1920.

Stuke, H. *Philosophie der Tat*. *Studien zur Verwirklichung der Philosophie bei den Junghegelianern und den wahren Sozialisten*, Stuttgart, 1963.

(C) BRUNO BAUER

TEXTS

Bauer, B. *Kritik der evangelischen Geschichte der Synoptiker*, 3 vol., Leipzig, 1841–2.

Bauer, B. *Die Posaune des jüngsten Gerichts über Hegel den Atheisten und Antichristen*, Leipzig, 1841, reprinted in *Die Hegelsche Linke*, ed. K. Löwith, Stuttgart, 1962.

Bauer, B. *Die Judenfrage*, Braunschweig, 1843.

Bauer, B. *Das entdeckte Christentum*, Zürich and Winterthur, 1843, ed. E. Barnikol, Jena, 1927.

COMMENTARIES

Barnikol, E. 'Bruno Bauers Kampf gegen Religion und Christentum', in *Zeitschrift für Kirchengeschichte*, vol. 46, 1928.

Bergh van Eysinga, G. A. van den, 'Die Tätigkeit von Bruno Bauer 1839–42', in *Annali*, VI, Milan, 1964.

Cesa, C. 'Bruno Bauer e la filosofia dell'autoscienza (1841–43)', in *Giornale Critico della Filosofia Italiana*, Firenze, 1960.

Gebhardt, J. 'Karl Marx und Bruno Bauer', in *Politische Ordnung und menschliche Existenz*, Festgabe für E. Voegelin, Munich, 1962.

Hertz-Eichenrode, D. *Der Junghegelianer Bruno Bauer im Vormärz*, Berlin, 1959.

Kegel, M. *Bruno Bauer und seine Theorien über die Entstehung des Christentums*, Leipzig, 1908.

(D) FEUERBACH

TEXTS

Feuerbach, L. *Sämtliche Werke*, ed. W. Bolin and F. Jodl, 2nd ed., Stuttgart, 1959.

M

TRANSLATIONS

Feuerbach, L. *Essence of Christianity*, trans. Marian Evans, London, 1853.
Feuerbach, L. *Manifestes philosophiques*, trans. L. Althausser, Paris, 1960.

COMMENTARIES

Arvon, H. *Ludwig Feuerbach, ou la transformation du sacré*, Paris, 1957.
Bockmühl, K. *Leiblichkeit und Gesellschaft. Studien zur Religionskritik und Anthropologie von Feuerbach und Marx*, Göttingen, 1961.
Dicke, G. *Der Identitätsgedanke bei Feuerbach und Marx*, Köln, 1960.
Lange, M. 'Ludwig Feuerbach und der junge Marx', Introduction to *Ludwig Feuerbach: Kleine philosophische Schriften*, Leipzig, 1950.
Rawidowicz, S. *Ludwig Feuerbachs Philosophie*, Berlin, 1931.

(E) STIRNER

TEXTS

Stirner, M. *Kleinere Schriften, . . . aus den Jahren 1842-47*, ed. J. Mackay, Berlin, 1898.
Stirner, M. *Der Einzige und sein Eigentum*, Leipzig, 1845.

TRANSLATIONS

Stirner, M. *The Ego and His Own*, trans. S. T. Byington, London, 1912.

COMMENTARIES

Arvon, H. *Aux sources de l'existentialisme, Max Stirner*, Paris, 1954.
Basch, V. *L'Individualisme anarchiste, Max Stirner*, Paris, 1904.
Mackay, J. *Max Stirner. Sein Leben und sein Werk*, Berlin, 1898.

(F) HESS

TEXTS

Hess, M. *Briefwechsel*, ed. Silberner, The Hague, 1959.
Hess, M. *Philosophische und sozialistische Aufsätze, 1837-1850*, ed. Cornu und Mönke, Berlin, 1961.

COMMENTARIES

Berlin, I. *The Life and Opinions of M. Hess*, 1959.
Cornu, A. *Moses Hess et la gauche hégélienne*, Paris, 1934.
Goitein, I. *Probleme der Gesellschaft und des Staates bei Moses Hess*, Leipzig, 1931.

Lukács, G. ' M. Hess und die Probleme der idealistischen Dialektik ', in *Archiv für die Geschichte des Sozialismus und der Arbeiterbewegung*, vol. 12, Leipzig, 1926.

Silberner, E. ' Der junge Moses Hess im Lichte bisher unerschlossener Quellen ', in *International Review for Social History*, vol. 3, Assen, 1958.

Silberner, E. ' Die Tätigkeit von Moses Hess 1841–43 ', in *Annali*, Milan, 1963.

Silberner, E. *Moses Hess*, Leiden, 1966.

Zlocisti, T. *Moses Hess, Vorkämpfer des Sozialismus und des Zionismus*, 2nd ed., Berlin, 1921.

(G) MARX

TEXTS

Marx–Engels, *Gesamtausgabe*, Berlin, 1927 ff.

Marx–Engels, *Werke*, Berlin, 1957 ff.

Marx, K. *Frühe Schriften*, Stuttgart, 1962 ff.

TRANSLATIONS

Marx, K. *Selected Writings in Sociology and Social Philosophy*, ed. Bottomore and Rubel, London 1956.

Marx, K. *Early Writings*, ed. Botomore, London, 1963.

Marx, K. *The Holy Family*, trans. Dixon, Moscow, 1956.

Marx, K. *German Ideology*, trans. Pascal, London, 1965.

COMMENTARIES

Adams, H. *Kárl Marx in his Earlier Writings*, London, 1940.

Avineri, S. *The Social and Political Thought of Karl Marx*, Cambridge, 1968.

Barth, H. *Wahrheit und Ideologie*, Zürich, 1945.

Bekker, K. *Marx philosophische Entwicklung. Sein Verhältnis zu Hegel*, Basel, 1940.

Berlin, I. *Karl Marx*, 3rd ed., London, 1963.

Calvez, J. Y. *La Pensée de Karl Marx*, Paris, 1956.

Cornu, A. *Karl Marx et Friedrich Engels, leur vie et leur œuvre*. Paris, 1955 f.

Cottier, G. *L'Athéisme du jeune Marx, ses origines hégéliennes*, Paris, 1959.

Delfgaauw, *The Young Marx*, trans. Schütz and Redfern, London, 1967.

Dupré, L. *Philosophical Foundations of Marxism*, New York, 1966.

Friedrich, M. *Philosophie und Ökonomie beim jungen Marx*, Berlin, 1960.

Hippolyte, J. *Études sur Marx et Hegel*, Paris, 1955.

Kamenka, E. *Ethical Foundations of Marxism*, London, 1962.

Popitz, H. *Der entfremdete Mensch*, Basel, 1953.

Rubel, M. *Karl Marx. Essai de biographie intellectuelle*, Paris, 1957.

Thier, E. *Das Menschenbild des jungen Marx*, Göttingen, 1957.

Tucker, R. *Philosophy and Myth in Karl Marx*, Cambridge, 1961.

Wackenheim, C. *La Faillite de la religion d'après Karl Marx*, Paris, 1963.

(H) RUGE

Arnold Ruges Briefwechsel und Tagebuchblätter 1825-1880, ed. Paul Nerrlich, 2 vols., Berlin, 1886.

A. Ruge, *Zwei Jahre in Paris*, Leipzig, 1846.

A. Ruge, *Sämtliche Werke*, Mannheim, 1847.

INDEX